Advance] Buddha

"A profound integration of clarity, heart, and grounded practice. Stephen is able to write with great precision and simplicity about far-reaching transformative processes. He is also deeply realized himself and can write from his own direct experience. It's a fantastic, amazing book!"

—Rick Hanson, PhD, psychologist and *NYT* bestselling author of *Buddha's Brain*

"Written from deep personal wisdom, *Buddha's Heart* expertly addresses key obstacles that block many people from accessing and opening to their true nature. Through clear and careful elucidation and instruction, Stephen brings these universal and timeless teachings to life."

—Jud Brewer, MD, PhD, Director of Research and Innovation, Mindfulness Center at Brown; Associate Professor in Psychiatry, School of Medicine, Brown University; and author of *The Craving Mind*

"A profoundly original and intimate presentation of awakening through Buddhist heart practices. Stephen's framing of classical Theravada teachings will inspire novice and experienced practitioners alike to explore heretofore unfathomed depths of their own tender hearts."

—Karin Meyers, PhD, Academic Director, Mangalam Research Center for Buddhist Languages

"A deep dive into the heart of who we truly are. Stephen offers us wise words and a host of nourishing Buddhist heart practices from the insight meditation tradition as doorways to awakening."

—Loch Kelly, meditation teacher, psychotherapist, and author of *The Way of Effortless Mindfulness*

"*Buddha's Heart* offers practices that orient us toward awakening the heart and give us glimpses of our true nature, our innate goodness. Stephen gives us a framework for seeing the way our psychological selves can react to Buddhist teachings. This book in itself is rich in generosity and love."

—June Kramer, MD, psychiatrist and psychoanalyst

"A thorough and inspiring step-by-step walk-through of just what the subtitle says: a meditation practice for developing well-being, love, and empathy. The experienced as well as the inexperienced meditator can reap a useful harvest from these pages."

—David Chadwick, editor of *Zen Is Right Here* and author of *Crooked Cucumber*

"Stephen draws on his extensive experience as a practitioner and teacher to offer the Buddhist heart meditations. Unlike much Western instruction, ethical preparation is at the fore, with the precepts and psychological interrogation used to gently prompt self-reflection and resolve obstacles. The result is a balanced and manageable guide to an extensive and profound practice."

—Kate Crosby, PhD, Professor of Buddhist Studies, King's College London, and author of *Esoteric Theravada*, UK

"Reading this book, a concise and practical guide to the *brahma-vihāras* of the Theravada Buddhist traditions, is like opening a bag of vacuum-packed tea, the surprising fullness of its contents belied by its small size."

—Charles Hallisey, MDiv, PhD, Harvard Divinity School

"*Buddha's Heart* is written from a place of authentic knowing and direct experience, rather than as an academic study. Both beginning and advanced students of spirituality and meditation would benefit from reviewing this book, which presents many core concepts with simple yet clear articulation."

—Heather C. Young, clinical psychologist and meditation teacher

"Stephen's rendering of these powerful heart meditations artfully blends the depth of traditional Buddhism with the insights of modern psychology. He offers a profound yet accessible perspective, rooted in a lifetime of dedicated personal practice and teaching."

—Steve James, educator, founder of the Movement Koan Method, and host of *The Guru Viking Podcast*

"A beautifully written book. The meditations offered strengthen the union between the body, the mind, the heart, and the spirit."

—The Rev. Katherine R. O'Connell, PhD, psychologist

"The strength of Stephen's approach is the identification of mental resistances to the wholesome heart qualities and the provision of how to overcome them by using manageable, useful exercises.

It is so refreshing to read about the importance of the heart and heart area in meditation practices, which is informed by Stephen's practice in a range of meditation traditions."

—Pyi Phyo Kyaw, PhD, Dean of Academic Affairs, Shan State Buddhist University, Myanmar

"This accessible but multilayered book invites us to return again and again to our own direct experience—to investigate our hearts, to taste and know the flavor of reality as it is, to trust the teachings and the profundity they hold for each of us, and to believe profound awakening is possible in a deeply deluded world."

—Laura Hauer, Executive Director, Cloud Mountain Retreat Center

"Reading *Buddha's Heart* felt like returning home to what is most true. Stephen's clear, concise approach to these ancient practices addresses both their psychological and spiritual aspects."

—Claire Charney, MSW, LICSW

"Whereas most Buddhist teachers focus their teaching upon the belly and head centers, Stephen draws our attention to the heart—this most subtle and central center of Being. He gently, but surely, guides us through ancient practices for developing qualities essential for living a full and compassionate life in this world."

—The Rev. Kevin G. Thew Forrester, PhD, St. Stephen's Episcopal Parish

"For the beginner, *Buddha's Heart* lays out a clear path of heart practice. For those with more experience, the beautiful and direct description of the final understandings and experiences of the path has the potential to clarify experiences as well as open new doors. It is unique and speaks with a grace, eloquence, and thoroughness seldom found."

—**Susie Harrington, meditation teacher, Desert Dharma**

"As a practicing monk at Pa-Auk Forest Monastery, I regularly turn to Stephen's teachings to gain clear and comprehensive explanations of Buddhist practice and meditations. With practices of the *brahmavihāras* (literally, "the dwelling place of the gods") to a description of *nibbāna* itself, this book is a gem for practitioners new and old."

—**Ñānavira, Matthew Buckley, Buddhist monk, Myanmar**

"A rare gem that masterfully guides the practitioner through a detailed and clear path to opening the heart while pointing out common and subtle resistances by the ego."

—**Andrea Serafino, mindfulness teacher and Jhāna Retreat founder, Italy**

"Pure inspiration and hope! *Buddha's Heart* leaves you with a desire to engage deep inner exploration, and it's a perfect guide to illuminate your inner light and joyous heart!"

—**Thomas Jedensjo, senior meditation student, Sweden**

"Meaningful both as a guide to a set of invaluable practices and as a source of inspiration to those of us seeking to engage with Buddhist teachings as a part of everyday life, *Buddha's Heart* left me feeling motivated and empowered to engage with these practices on a deeper level, an effect I am sure it will have on many readers."

—Jonathan Lilly, PhD, research scientist

"This is a beautifully written guide that describes how the Buddhist path can bring authentic inner peace and unconditioned happiness. Studying the 'immeasurables,' Stephen invites us to move from a poverty of grasping to the rich suchness of being."

—Judy F. Kennedy, PhD, psychologist and business consultant

"A lucid, step-by-step, practical manual of *brahmavihāra* meditations for both beginner and seasoned practitioners, searching for Absolute truth."

—Tomislav Marić, anthropologist, educator, and senior meditation student, UK

"An invaluable, concise manual to experiencing the qualities and subtleties of the heart."

—Andrea Magoni, senior meditation student, Italy

BUDDHA'S
HEART

BUDDHA'S HEART

*Meditation Practice
for Developing
Well-Being, Love,
and Empathy*

Stephen Snyder

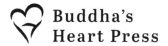 Buddha's
Heart Press

Buddha's Heart Press
www.awakeningdharma.org

Library of Congress Control Number: 2020916269
ISBN 978-1-7347810-2-1 (paperback)
ISBN 978-1-7347810-3-8 (e-book)

Editing by Erin Parker
Proofreading by Lynn Slobogian
Cover and interior design by Jazmin Welch
E-book production by Bookmobile
Project management by Carra Simpson

*I dedicate this book to Shakyamuni
Buddha for the brilliant shining light of his
realization and teaching.
The light of realization shines always
in this very moment.*

Contents

Foreword

OVER THE COURSE of two and a half thousand years, as the teachings of its founder, Siddhartha Gautama, spread and flourished throughout Asia and eventually to the Western world, Buddhism has evolved to adapt and integrate with the various cultures it has encountered. Today Buddhism comprises a rich family of traditions and a diversity of aims and practices. Even within a single Buddhist tradition can be found a range of understandings and views about the goal and the proper way to attain it.

Though understandings of the path to enlightenment and liberation vary, and meditation practices can be found in many forms, most Buddhist contemplative traditions share in emphasizing a few core elements. They all essentially aim to cultivate foundational qualities of the heart and mind, wholesome qualities that support us to live in a way that creates ever-less suffering and more happiness and well-being, for others and ourselves.

The methods may vary but these essential elements are shared in common: loving-kindness, compassion, and other aspects of a loving heart; mindfulness; mental stability; clarity; equanimity; and insight. Any practices that cultivate these can lead one to liberation.

Buddha's Heart presents a powerful and readily accessible path of practice to realize and deepen all these wholesome qualities, a thorough system for steadying the mind, opening the heart, and realizing with insight the potential within each of us for profound clarity, wisdom, and love.

Beginning with a foundation of ethical conduct, practical exercises are offered for deepening concentration, touching profound places of love and compassion lying within each of us, and realizing the nature of our own being.

The strength of this system lies in its dual approach. It offers practical, guided practices for cultivating positive, wholesome dharma qualities and also seeks to address and remove negative, unwholesome self-views that can block access to those qualities. We must nurture the positive qualities we wish to develop and also shine the light of awareness on challenging places of resistance that inhibit these qualities from being expressed.

Along with practices for building mindfulness, concentration, insight, and a good heart, the reader is guided through a series of reflections aimed at uncovering and letting go of the blocks that can bind us in suffering. Practical reflections are offered to explore areas of negative thought patterns and views, resistance, and blockages, all of which hold back the natural expression of our innate goodness.

You may wish to work systematically from the beginning through the entire course of meditations and reflections. Or you could begin anywhere you are drawn, as you choose, taking as much time as you wish with each section and practice. You can engage fully with this system as the entirety of your meditation practice or use various aspects to supplement other practices you are engaged in. You may discover whole new directions to explore in your meditation.

Whether you are a beginning meditator or seasoned practitioner, you will find a full system that can take you from the initial stages of meditation to deep stages of self-realization.

Richard Shankman
Author, *The Experience of Samadhi* and *The Art and Skill of Buddhist Meditation*

Introduction

NAVIGATING DAILY LIFE has never been more complicated. Life's unrelenting demands disturb our inner state of peaceful quiet. Constant electronic interruptions can lead to feeling hopeless, helpless, and without inner support. There is an alternative to feeling overwrought by life. We can turn inward to engage in soothing, nourishing Buddhist heart practices that feed our soul. These ancient heart meditations allow us to gently, lovingly touch our contracted, wounded hearts while opening to the flow of the unconditioned heart qualities of our deeper nature. Engaging a heart meditation means following a formula to relax our learned resistances to

I have found heart practices to be a balm for the soul, as well as a portal to spiritual awakening and deepening self-realization.

heart qualities, such as compassion, while opening to receive compassion for ourselves and ultimately directing it for the benefit of others. I have found heart practices to be a balm for the soul, as well as a portal to spiritual awakening and deepening self-realization. So have many of my students. As the world descends into increasing overstimulation by nonstop news and constant social media updates, it becomes critical to find the quiet, nurturing comfort afforded by the heart practices in this book—contacting and cultivating a deeply felt sense of our undivided wholeness with all other beings. Ongoing contact with the undivided heart connection with all living beings provides an unshakable knowing that we are never truly isolated or alone.

I first discovered the Buddhist heart meditations in the 1990s. At the time, there were no books on the topic that I could find. I met someone who had learned the practices while spending time in an Asian monastery. I was clumsy with the meditations to start but could feel a growing connection with my own heart. At that point in my life, I saw myself as a head and belly practitioner, meaning I had intellectual understanding and a developed intuitive knowing in my belly. But my heart area was fairly inaccessible to me. I eventually learned that going deep in my meditation (belly) and conceptualizing the emotional issues (head) were insufficient ways to work with emotional issues that were arising in my life. If I did not invite the vulnerability of my heart, relief escaped me. In the succeeding years, I have found comfort by turning to these heart practices when I feel disconnected from my deepest self, particularly at times of emotional turmoil in my life.

I did not deeply undertake these heart practices on retreat until 2004. During a two-month retreat, with the support of my teacher, the Venerable Pa Auk Sayadaw, I engaged these practices to a high level of absorption concentration, called *jhāna*. The practices penetrated not only my consciousness but also the hidden recesses of my heart, which opened and were awakened through the intensity of the *jhāna* level of concentration meditation. This intensely profound level of accessing these unconditioned heart qualities changed me. I knew the deep connection ever present with all living beings. This gave me comfort. Intimately knowing this unbroken connection with all life, I could readily open to receive the universal heart qualities described in this book.

After the two-month retreat with the Venerable Pa Auk Sayadaw, he encouraged me and another senior student to write a book, *Practicing the Jhānas*. The Sayadaw felt that it would be compelling to others to learn about the ancient meditations from the modern perspective of an accomplished Western practitioner. He invited me to teach with him on a retreat in 2006, which included him observing my one-on-one interviews with students. After that retreat, he authorized me as one of the first Western lay teachers in his lineage.

Teaching and guiding students on retreat, I began to see that several conditions were preventing them from deeply accessing these purification-of-heart practices: psychological blocks and resistances, the deeply held belief in a separate self, and a perspective that these heart states were simply emotions. I wrote this book to address these obstacles and share my own practice experiences in hopes of helping novice and experienced meditators alike to open more fully to these sublime, wholesome heart qualities.

In any building project, a stable, secure foundation is needed. Chapter 1, "Heart's View," orients us to the reality of our deepest true nature and explains why we tend to overlook the warmhearted support available in the underlying connection with all living beings. We then shift to preparations for the heart meditations to come. The second chapter, "Wholesome Support," is an in-depth exploration of Buddhist precepts that make us more skillful in our actions, which minimizes remorse and regret. In Chapter 3, we learn to anchor our practice in concentration meditation, specifically mindfulness of breathing. Concentration meditation is the fuel that powers our journey into the profound depths of our heart. The "Foundation" section will likely be a refresher for the experienced meditators.

The heart meditations presented in the next section are traditional Buddhist meditations handed down from teacher to student for over 2,500 years. These timeless, and timely, meditations are available to anyone with the desire to uncover the precious jewel of love, and soften and heal their contracted, wounded hearts. Each meditation in Chapters 4 through 8—Innate Goodness, *Upekkhā*: Equanimity, *Muditā*: Empathetic Joy, *Karuṇā*: Compassion, and *Mettā*: Loving-Kindness—opens us to a different heart resonance, exposing its resistances, hurts, and unimaginable curative beauty. Recognizing and understanding resistances (such as anger, hatred, and envy) is a crucial part of the process that is explored in a unique way in this section of the book. When we have the freedom, the inner permission, to *feel* these negative emotions without acting upon them, they lose most of their unconscious power that otherwise suppresses the tender heart qualities highlighted by these meditations.

For the experienced meditator, there is a deepening progression of these heart meditations. Each heart meditation can expand to the point that we drop our perception of being a body or mind and our awareness rests in, and as, each pure heart quality. Steeping in our pure, radiant heart profoundly alters our understanding of who and what we are. It also opens us to deepening our personal and love relationships through sharing our increasingly undefended heart.

Novice and expert alike will find the practices in "Heart Purifying" helpful for directing meditative awareness to gratitude for life's blessings (Chapter 9), offering forgiveness to ourselves and others, and opening ourselves to the hurt places we hold tightly closed in protection (Chapter 10). Chapter 11 then invites all readers deeper into the undivided Oneness of reality, highlighting the wholeness embracing each of us.

Finally, in "Culmination," we see the life-altering results of engaging these practices and meditations. Chapter 12 shows how these heart qualities can, and will, spontaneously arise to perfectly meet suffering in the world. This is the natural functioning of the heart's wisdom. We then explore, in Chapter 13, the journey from deep in the Absolute realm through formless reality through experiences of absence of self and no-self to our everyday world. Understanding this journey of reality helps us to know, for ourselves, that these heart qualities originate from an unconditioned, infinite source.

I suggest you initially read the book from start to finish with an open heart and mind. Allow each section and chapter to fully land in you. Once you complete the book, begin the meditations or practices that call to you or to which you are directed by your teacher. Take your time with each meditation and exercise. Be open and curious without expecting or directing toward any specific result. Let yourself be steeped in the heart wisdom and joy of each practice. I encourage you to keep a journal to record what you learn about each meditation practice and which resistances you meet as well as how you are affected and changed.

Finally, allow these practices to work in you and on you. Take a few weeks or a month to dive deeply into each practice and meditation. Follow the path where these meditations lead without any expectation. Thoroughly review your life for people and things for which to offer sincere gratitude. Be open, tender, and willing to make contact with the hurt in your heart as you sincerely offer forgiveness to yourself and

The greater your willingness to be impacted and changed, the deeper your transformation will be. The more tender your heart becomes, the more resilient, flexible, and responsive you will be. Ironically, the more authentically vulnerable we become, the safer and more protected we are.

others. Be willing to be new to yourself as your tender heart guides and nourishes you.

I recommend that each reader and practitioner allow themselves to be as soft and permeable as possible while engaging with these practices. The greater your willingness to be impacted and changed, the deeper your transformation will be. The more tender your heart becomes, the more resilient, flexible, and responsive you will be. Ironically, the more authentically vulnerable we become, the safer and more protected we are. When we feel safe, supported by our hearts, what would have once wounded our hearts passes through without landing. This is because we can feel more deeply, with fewer historic contractions, and can have a response that is true, in this moment, for us.

Foundation

WE WILL BEGIN OUR JOURNEY into the depths of our heart by exploring the heart's view in Chapter 1. We began this life in an indivisible Oneness. This was our early life's connection to the source of all reality. The loss, or diminishment, of this intimate connection propelled us to seek love from caregivers, family, and friends through close relationships. While these people can offer care and love, they cannot answer our inner call to return to Unity with the Source. I expect this chapter will intuitively resonate with many readers. This resonance strengthens the inner confidence that we are welcomed and loved by the Source. Knowing we are connected, included, and lovingly held allows us to open our tender hearts more deeply in the heart meditations.

We use the Buddhist precepts as a guide for living as clear and clean a life as possible. The precepts codify the natural functioning of the Source, the Absolute realm, as it animates every aspect of life. In Chapter 2, these are presented from the outer view, which is the worldly view; the inner view, which reveals our personality inclinations and psychological workings; and the secret view, which is anchored and expresses the undivided connection with the Source, the Absolute realm. Including the precepts in your daily and retreat life supports more wholesome living in attunement with our deepest awake nature.

Another important support for the Buddha's Heart practices is concentration meditation, the focus of Chapter 3. Concentration is a foundational meditation practice. Virtually every major religion or spiritual group has a form of concentration meditation, which involves holding one meditative object in awareness to the exclusion of all else. Concentration meditation develops our ability to maintain awareness on a meditative object without significant interruption, while promoting greater relaxation and ease. Becoming familiar with this meditation and practicing it regularly will let you dive deeper into the meditations in this book and in your usual practices.

1

Heart's View

WHEN WE ARE BORN, we have a newborn's connection to our deepest nature, our true self, what I am calling the "Presence of the Absolute." The Absolute realm is the source of all phenomenon, all life. Babies' connection to the Presence of the Absolute is not an *awakened knowing*, as can happen in the mature unfolding of a spiritual practice or life. The child's contact is a connection with the Source, the Absolute realm, which has not yet been disrupted or broken by the personality's development.

As babies develop a mentally structured personality, they are increasingly socializing with their birth family and caregiver. Babies initially feel connected with all people in their world by an undivided wholeness called "dual unity" in psychology. To learn more about this process, read *The Psychological Birth of the Human Infant* by Margaret S. Mahler, Fred Pine, and Anni Bergman.

During the dual unity phase of infant development, babies do not, and cannot, differentiate between themselves and their caregivers. This phase is a merged oneness of awareness and identity for the baby. It is also a union of Oneness with the Presence quality of the Absolute realm.

Over time, as babies begin to establish a psychologically structured personality, the perception of the dual unity fades. The dual unity fading signals a turning away from connection with the Presence of the Absolute. In time, as the personality becomes more established, and the child's identity is increasingly invested in their personality, the experience of the connection with the Presence fades from memory. Some adults seem to have a faint recollection of this intimate childhood connection with the Presence; others do not.

As the inner connection with the Presence of the Absolute fades, there develops an inner yearning, a heart longing to return to that undivided unity with the Presence. The heart longing is not specifically for the Presence of the Absolute. It is an unspecified longing for unbreakable love. Along with this heart yearning, there is a knowing of being disconnected, adrift in life with a persistent feeling of irretrievable loss. This perception of lingering loss leaves most of us with a deep, unquenchable longing for love. We seek to reestablish the satisfying merging love with a precious other.

The longing for love propels us to locate love outside of ourselves. We look to others to not only witness our deep longing, our increasing desperation, but to completely satisfy the empty ache of our hearts. When we secure a love interest, we feel hopeful that our needs will be met, our heart aches soothed. The truth is that no other person can either fully know the longing of our heart or fill that ache. Ultimately, we experience a deeper, agonizing loss when we finally conclude our love interest is unable to satisfy our deep longing. Discovering that our love interest cannot resolve our yearning for connection and wholeness compels many people to seek a different love interest who will soothe this deep heart ache. Yearning can also be felt as a gnawing inner hunger. This inner hunger can only be quenched by the love of the Absolute. Love is the viscosity, the medium of the Presence of the Absolute. We try to fill our heart's hunger with the love of a special other, with food or drink, with mind-numbing intoxicants, or with excessive or inappropriate sexual relationships. These distractions will never satisfy the heart's longing, just temporarily numb it from our view.

There is only one way to fill this lifelong heart ache—awakening to the Presence of the Absolute as your core identity. This hunger for love begins to be satisfied by a First Awakening. A First Awakening is an awakening to unending love, marked by a transparency of ego. In a First Awakening, consciousness merges with the ever-present Awakeness that is the Presence of the Absolute. This awakening will likely be the first time our heart's longing feels quenched and soothed. A First Awakening will also offer a path to deeply satisfying, real, unconditioned, accepting love. I have included the experience of my First Awakening in Chapter 11, "Oneness of Reality," to illustrate how this can unfold.

The Presence of the Absolute has a medium, a felt perception, of fulfilled love. Fulfilled love is the inner quality, the aliveness, the tenderness, the strength that infuses and animates all life. This means that everything we can see, hear, or touch is composed of this profoundly satisfying love. When we are awakened to this love, and in ongoing contact with it, our hearts will be authentically affected. This inclusive love is the deeply welcoming acceptance of the Presence. Sustained contact with universal love begins

It is through sustained connection with the Presence of the Absolute that our lifelong heart ache feels seen and rests in ease.

the journey of quenching our yearning. It satisfies our inner hunger, our heart's deepest ache and longing.

It is through sustained connection with the Presence of the Absolute that our lifelong heart ache feels seen and rests in ease. As our connection with the Presence deepens and becomes sustaining, we loosen our grip on our identification with the heart's ache, and our compulsive behaviors relax. Our self-definition shifts to the Presence as our core identity. With sustained contact with the love of the Presence, our personality's foundation begins to shift from the heart's ache to the infinite love of the Presence—our true, authentic identity. The true identity of the Presence is your birthright.

This is why learning, practicing, and integrating the deep heart meditations in this book are so vital to our spiritual maturation. Each meditation opens a different quality of our true nature in our heart while deepening contact and connection with the Presence of the Absolute.

2

Wholesome Support

SĪLA (WHOLESOMENESS) is an important anchor for our journey into the Buddha's Heart. "Wholesomeness" means acting from a place that is wholehearted and authentic. Wholesomeness is reviewing your intentions and reflecting upon whether your outer behavior matches your inner understanding. It is being as true a human being as possible.

Sīla is often translated as "morality" or "ethics," but I have used "wholesomeness" throughout my teaching career. With "ethics" and "morality," there is an implicit judgment, whereas with "wholesomeness," there is little to no judgment, which makes the concept more approachable for students.

The process of living wholesomely begins with the request to take refuge in the the Buddha, the Dhamma (Dharma), and the Saṅgha. In taking refuge, we are both seeking support for our spiritual practice and recognizing the Buddha, Dhamma, and Saṅgha. The refuges are a location where we can rest when weary. We carry them with us as inspiration for our unfolding realization. When I refer to the Buddha, I am referring to both the historical Buddha—Shakyamuni—and the potential of each of us to be a fully functioning, self-realized Buddha. *Dhamma* is usually translated as "teaching," and it should be presented in a manner that conveys the truthfulness of the practices as well as their direct applicability to our day-to-day personal lives. *Saṅgha* is translated as "community." This means the local and international community of Buddhist practitioners engaging in the various practices and committing themselves to wholesome living while doing as little harm in their lives as possible. *Saṅgha* includes laypeople as well as monastics.

If you are deeply sincere in your request to take refuge and you ask three times, it is tradition that the teacher cannot refuse you. Once we have asked, in our own words, to take refuge three times, it is customary on meditation retreats to take the precepts, which are also included in *sīla*. The Buddhist precepts are wholesome guides or measures that gauge the effects of our behavior, and they are used as respite and support for the journey of exploration into our deepest interiority. In Theravada Buddhism, the precepts are chanted by Buddhists around the world in Pali, the language of the Buddha's day.

In this chapter, I will present the precepts in English and present the outer, inner, and secret understanding of each one. The outer is the most apparent, secular understanding. The inner aspect of the precepts highlights the relationship of thought and emotion with the intent of the precept. The secret knowing is from the perspective of our meditative understanding. As our meditation deepens, our intuitive knowing deepens, too, as we make deeper contact with the Presence of the Absolute. The secret meaning helps us navigate life by clarifying our understanding of the precepts while living from, and expressing, our level of intuitive understanding.

First Precept: "I undertake the precept to refrain from killing living beings."

Outer: The outer understanding is that we will not end life. This means refraining from knowingly killing other beings. In its application, our behavior needs to be congruent with our values and also support our lives, which need sustenance. Simply by living and eating, we will take life. We will inadvertently kill insects and life forms that are unseen. Moreover, we need to eat in order to survive. We will kill vegetables and possibly animals for our life to continue. Some of us will use humane means to collect and release insects outside and not simply kill them on sight as may be customary in our culture. Some people will feel most resonant with internal wholesomeness by refraining from eating meat. There is not one right answer to these issues of sustaining life. These are personal choices that we each must navigate, being as consistent as possible with our inner guidance and spiritual understanding.

Inner: The inner application of this precept is about monitoring the content of our thoughts. Internally we can be aware of—even know—our undivided connection with all of life and all living beings. When, in our thoughts, we view others as separate and foreign to us, we are trying to divide the quality of our deeper nature that is fully complete and incapable of division. We can recognize this thought pattern when we are being critical and disparaging of others. In trying to divide the wholeness of our true nature, we are prioritizing our personality over the inner knowing of complete unity.

Secret: Our deepest nature, that of Being—called "the Absolute" in Buddhism—is manifested as every living entity and life form. The reality is that all phenomena are of the identical substance as we are. When we prioritize our personality over the reality of Oneness, we reject our deepest truth by cutting ourselves off from deep connection with others. This is a kind of killing of the natural Presence and intelligent functioning of the Absolute.

Second Precept: "I undertake the precept to refrain from taking what is not given."

Outer: Refraining from taking what is not given, on its surface, means not stealing. This also means not helping ourselves to something that has not been freely and expressly offered. For example, we may see a bowl of candy sitting out. Presuming it is for all, we may take some. Applying this precept, we should confirm it is being offered to all before taking any. This approach allows us to be clear in our understanding and actions, and supports our being congruent with our values. It also minimizes the guilt or remorse we might feel later upon learning it was not being offered to us.

Inner: Inner appropriations usually show up as envy and jealousy. We see others' possessions, even their happiness, and want them for ourselves, to soothe our inner lack. This means we feel a deficiency without a clear means of satisfaction. We generally try to fill this need with material possessions. We think if we can just get this one item we are lacking, we will feel safe, fulfilled, and complete. Typically,

> *We are not enriched by accumulating more nor fulfilled by coveting others' possessions. When we are in touch with the natural way of the universe, everything is an undivided part of each of us. We are deeply content being who we are, as we are, with what we have.*

when we get the desired item, it immediately satisfies our inner hunger. Shortly, it shifts from being very satisfying to being ordinary, and we return to our feeling of lack. Our belief in our deficient state feels permanent, and the hunger for wholeness arises again.

Secret: We are an undivided part of the whole of the universe. It is impossible to be separated from the wholeness of the Absolute. We have never been split off, nor have we been cast out or rejected. Truthfully, we turned away from the Presence of the Absolute by investing in our personality as the sole view of reality. This is a core psychological belief. We want to invite greater acceptance of the Absolute as the Source and participate in the natural flow of the Absolute fulfilling our needs. We are not enriched by accumulating more nor fulfilled by coveting others' possessions. When we are in touch with the natural way of the universe, everything is an undivided part of each of us. We are deeply content being who we are, as we are, with what we have. What we need most will appear in our life in perfect timing and harmony. It will not necessarily be what we want, but it will be what we need. When we know the undivided nature of the universe for ourselves, we do not want for anything. What is needed appears. Trust arises from our contented, interconnected state. We see that what is right here, right now, is enough and we can be deeply satisfied.

Third Precept: "I undertake the precept to refrain from (all) sexual activity."

Outer: This precept is for retreats. On a retreat, all sexual activity ceases. We want to use the very potent energy we usually release in sex for our spiritual journey, deepening our unfolding toward realization. Cultivating this energy while on retreat is optimal.

For laypeople, applying this precept to daily life means using our sexual energy and sexuality responsibly—participating in sex consciously, deliberately, in wholesome, mutually beneficial ways. For some, this means enjoying sex in a committed relationship with one partner. For others, it means being responsible to our truth and to potential partners in expressing our sexuality with integrity.

Inner: Inner sexuality is a preoccupation with sex. Here we are looking at how we think about and idealize relationships and sex. We learn how much mental energy we spend on merged intimacy, sexual ideation/idealization, and fantasy, and how we may introduce envy and jealousy into relationships.

From a spiritual practice perspective, this precept teaches us to monitor our mentalizing to notice when we fantasize about wanting a partner who is unavailable. We can be in touch with a felt sense of lack and find ourselves mentally seeking someone to distract us from our feelings of insufficiency. This means we observe our thinking, our daydreams, our wanting for another to make us whole, accepted, and loved.

Secret: From the perspective of ultimate reality, we are deeply connected to the Presence of the Absolute, which includes all others. There is no perceived lack, no need to be seen, appreciated, or valued to feel our innate wholeness. Sexual activity with a committed partner is intimately life affirming. When we are deeply connected to another, there is no longing to use sexual activity to ward off feelings of neediness. Sexual activity, when we engage in it with a deep spiritual intent, can be an opportunity to deepen our awareness into the undivided quality of the Absolute through sustained intimate connection and bonding with another.

Fourth Precept: "I undertake the precept to refrain from false speech."

Outer: In a silent retreat setting, this is not a hard precept to keep. In normal life, this precept is an admonition to refrain from saying what you know to be false. The precept is encouraging us to speak our truth and relinquish gossip and idle talk. We are trying to avoid harming others or ourselves through speech. The precept points to our speaking heartfully without any level, or intent, of manipulation.

Inner: Internal false speech is typically self-talk. Self-talk is repeating our story internally to reassert and reify who we take ourselves to be. It is an attempt to shore up our sense of self, our personality. Internal false speech includes inner judgments we have toward ourselves and others. This internal false speech in psychology is called the "inner critic" or "superego." Simply put, the superego is an internalized personification of a parent or other influential person from our early childhood who directed our behavior in an effort to keep us safe.

We need to be diligent to not completely identify with these inner opinions and self-talk. When self-talk arises, we must learn to be as neutral toward it as possible. Then, we will become more open to our mysterious inner nature.

Secret: Our personal consciousness is an undivided whole with the awakened, fully self-aware consciousness. To truly refrain from all false speech is to only speak from, and as, this fully awake consciousness to the extent it is activated and functioning. This means we use language that is inclusive rather than divisive. We function and speak more from our deepest love, the love of the Absolute or the divine. We offer kindness, acceptance, and appreciation to others as we see them as ourselves. We are all part of the Absolute's glorious, undivided, loving wholeness.

Fifth Precept: "I undertake the precept to refrain from taking intoxicants, which cloud the mind and cause heedlessness."

Outer: On retreat, we do not consume intoxicants. Neither alcohol nor nonprescription drugs are permitted. We seek to be in a more natural, aware state of mind. We choose not to act from the effects of mind-altering substances. We want our mind in its most unaltered state to open to, and be with, our deepest nature.

Inner: There are many ways we cloud our minds, even without using intoxicants. Our inner talk, the constant narrative of every aspect of our life, is a kind of intoxicant. We narrate our life to reaffirm our belief in apparent inner and outer reality. This precept is encouraging us to loosen our grip on this inner narrative, to invite greater awareness of the wholeness of our deeper nature. We do this to touch into and guide our unfolding process.

Secret: We use our memories, thoughts, body image, and self-image to tell ourselves the story of who we are. What is problematic about this is the unrelenting repetition of these memories, thoughts, and images, and the investment we make in being only this particular person with a particular, unchanging self-identity. This precept encourages us to take a step away from these limiting self-beliefs and identities. Being on the spiritual journey, we explore what it is like to simply be, without so much self-definition or allegiance to our mentalized identity.

Sixth Precept: "I undertake the precept to refrain from taking food at improper times (after midday)."

Outer: On traditional Buddhist retreats, in the Theravada Buddhist tradition, food is not served after the midday meal. This encourages modesty toward craving and satisfaction with what is received. It helps develop acceptance and deconstructs our elaborate mental process of wanting, greed, or craving.

Inner: One of the beliefs we hold closest is that there will never be enough food or love available to us; we are truly, fundamentally lacking. This feeling of deficiency stems from our loss of contact with the Presence of the Absolute, and we can experience desperation as a sense of craving, a hollowness within. We conclude if we do not ensure we secure enough sustenance for ourselves, we will probably die. This precept helps us confront this part of an unseen survival drive. We learn we can survive well on two meals a day by ceasing to eat after midday. We learn we can be content, and feel whole, even when hunger is present.

Secret: Everything we perceive is a part of an undivided wholeness, a wholesome wholeness. Everything we need is always present and available to, and for, us. There is no lack in ultimate reality, the Absolute. This precept supports our intimacy with this wholeness. It encourages us to be content, even in the face of gnawing need. We can be closely aware of our need yet not let it be aroused to the point of desperation. We can feel need and concurrently feel the wholeness that contains all and meets all needs perfectly. This unbroken wholeness supports us resting contentedly in our deepest nature and not seeking anything.

Seventh Precept: "I undertake the precept to refrain from dancing, singing, enjoying music and shows, and from the use of garlands, perfumes, cosmetics, adornments, and ornaments."

Outer: As most Buddhist retreats are silent, we choose to not excite the mind with various forms of entertainment. We also refrain from needing to beautify ourselves, to decorate ourselves principally for others with perfumes, cosmetics, and any other adornments.

Inner: Refraining from entertainment on retreat helps us to be with our inner silence, our deeper nature. A common function of social activity is distracting us from self-examination, taking us away from the inner deficiency of incompleteness. Refraining from beautifying ourselves challenges our self-image. It also supports us being wholesomely plain while on retreat.

Secret: Through our behavior and clothing, we encourage others to see us a particular way and reflect our self-image. The question is: Who are we without all the outward displays of beauty? How do we know who we are unless we refrain from outward-oriented displays through the right clothes, right hairstyle, the right cologne or perfume? This precept helps us cut through the exterior signs of self-ornamentation and draw our inner curiosity toward a deeper level of knowing who we are.

Eighth Precept: "I undertake the precept to refrain from using high and luxurious seats and beds."

Outer: Part of the Buddhist retreat experience is accepting what is offered as being sufficient for our needs. We only need room and board to sustain our meditation and spiritual practices. More than that is considered extravagant. We want to put down our expectations of opulence and accept what is sincerely offered.

Inner: Part of our self-image is a need to be seen as special, as deserving luxury. This can translate into constantly wanting an upgrade in convenience and comfort. This precept challenges that core wanting, the inner hunger pangs for more. We learn to accept what we are given and yet ensure we have what we need. We exercise wisdom to clarify what we really need versus what we believe we want. This practice cultivates a deeper acceptance of what is needed to be comfortable enough for the sustained inner journey.

Secret: In our deepest levels, we are content, welcoming, and always grateful for whatever we receive. Our personality deficiency—our belief in ourselves as a separate self—can make us feel a deep, insatiable hunger to be recognized as the most special. This can lead to a further longing for more than we are given in life. This precept helps us be with that deep deficiency and its inner hunger, without needing to change it. We can learn to feel, and be with, the hunger of wanting more while accepting what is earnestly offered.

3

Concentration Meditation

CONCENTRATION MEDITATION is a practice in which we prioritize one meditation object (often the breath) to the exclusion of everything else in our awareness. It was the first meditation the Buddha suggested to novices. He did this, in my view, because he knew that if we developed an ability to focus awareness, every meditation and spiritual practice would penetrate more deeply, its benefits realized.

Concentration meditation was my first meditative practice. I was able to secure one of the few books in English on Zen practice in 1975. It was called *The Three Pillars of Zen*. I used that book, along with *A Buddhist Bible* by Dwight Goddard, to commence my meditation practice. I began meditating for about five minutes per sitting. My mind simply could not rest and refrain from hyperactivity for more than five minutes. Over time, and with twice-daily meditation sessions, I relaxed sufficiently to be able to sit for thirty minutes or more.

From my first meditation, I knew I was finding my ground, my base for maturing and deepening my very beingness. I was unaware how this would happen even though I could feel the importance of meditation. A number of months later, I had coworkers approaching me to share how appreciative they were of my calmness and peaceful nature. I was surprised to hear this. I had not told them about my daily meditation. My coworkers were feeling and seeing a changing me. To me, this was irrefutable proof of the importance of spiritual practice and the benefits of concentration meditation.

In this chapter, we will develop concentration meditation practice as a support for the heart practices in the next section. The heart meditations in this book are in the spiritual territory of concentration meditation, as is mindfulness of breathing. Concentration meditation provides stability to penetrate our individual heart, opening to the ever-present universal awakened heart.

Concentration Meditation Practice

> Seat yourself in a comfortable position in a chair or on a meditation cushion.

> Take a few deep belly breaths, letting your awareness settle in your belly.

> Try to sit such that your legs are lower than your hips.

> Place your hands in your lap or high on your thighs.

> Close your eyes.

> Bring your awareness to the space between your nostrils and upper lip.

> Let your awareness rest on the breath as it enters and exits the body through your nostrils.

> Do not follow the breath into the body or away from the body. Stay focused exclusively on that area between the nostrils and upper lip.

> Maintain your attention on the breath to the exclusion of everything else arising in your awareness. Do not try to either push away or

> engage with thoughts, emotions, body activity, or memories.

> ❯ Just be with the natural breath.

> ❯ As your body and mind settle, your mind will feel it is beginning to unify and coalesce by being more serene, more peaceful.

Start out spending a minimum of ten minutes undertaking this meditation.

Being with the breath as it crosses between the nostrils and the upper lip is a practice you can do when you are waiting in a line or stopped at a traffic light. In other words, it is a meditation you can do anywhere since you are always breathing. Of course, you do not want to do it when you are actively driving or engaged in an activity in which safety requires your full attention.

Heart
Meditations

THROUGHOUT OUR LIVES, we receive feedback and judgments from others. When this feedback highlights our best sense of self, the person we feel we are, we are elated. We feel seen. Conversely, when we receive feedback or judgments that feel overly critical or that mistake who we feel we are, it leaves a heart wound. These accumulated wounds create a hardening and defensive contracting of our hearts. Our hearts become more defended, less open, and less available to ourselves and others. The heart meditations here not only soften and heal these contracted and wounded places but also open our awareness to the inherent profundity of our hearts.

In presenting these teachings, I have reorganized how and when each meditation is done. These heart meditations are often taught in this order: *mettā* (loving-kindness), *muditā* (empathetic joy), *karuṇā* (compassion), and *upekkhā* (equanimity). I believe the following revised order supports a deeper connection with the reality of our true nature and allows for a more thorough experience of each meditation while we witness its benefits: innate goodness, *upekkhā* (equanimity), *mudità* (empathetic joy), *karunā* (compassion), and *mettā* (loving-kindness).

The first meditation in this section is called "innate goodness." I have found that when students deepen connection with their innate goodness, it soothes the psychological needs and cravings of the personality by immediately counteracting the belief they are unlovable or unworthy of intimacy. In turn, this permits the student to penetrate each meditation more fully, which draws forward their true nature's heart qualities.

The second meditation in this section, *upekkhā* (equanimity), affords a closeness to the deeper reality of what is true. *Upekkhā* is about recognizing the inherent balance in whatever is happening. It touches the rightness of life as it is experienced. We develop greater acceptance of what is happening by trusting that there is a profound rightness here. This profound rightness provides a stability of ease upon which to explore and open to the other heart meditations.

We next shift to *mudità* (empathetic or sympathetic joy) practice. *Mudità* invites us to contact another's good fortune or joy. This takes us from *upekkhā*, steeping in equanimity/ harmony, the unity of all reality, to feeling pure joy for another. Pure joy for another connects our heart with the hearts of others. *Muditā* softens the barriers—the separating psychological walls—between us and others. When we feel joy in witnessing another's successes, we are also minimizing envy and jealousy. We feel happy that they are having good things happen.

We next shift to *karuṇā* (compassion) meditation. Contact with *karuṇā* teaches us to gently hold pain, distress, and suffering. We are not trying to remove our, or their, suffering. We are recognizing that suffering is a fundamental reality of human life. Yet we can help ourselves and others by holding suffering tenderly with openness. *Karuṇā* develops trust in the reality that life is unfolding exactly as it should. We each have suffering in our lives. This is a foundational truth. We will never eliminate all suffering. Since suffering exists, the skillfulness is in being present to suffering without becoming reactive or closing our hearts. *Karuṇā* develops the skill of being humanely present to all of reality.

Finally, we venture into *mettā* (loving-kindness), loving all others. Once we have the stability of equanimity, the connection of empathetic joy, and the holding support of compassion, we can more easily contact and express pure loving-kindness. By knowing the Oneness of all life, love can collect in our heart. *Mettā* passes this collected love through us as it reaches out to other living beings.

In these heart meditations, we orient toward a particular heart quality of our deeper nature. We learn the practice of each meditation, explore the common resistances, and see what is similar to the heart qualities we are accessing. Work carefully through the exercises. There is much that will be revealed. Assumptions and beliefs about these different heart qualities will surface as you are right here with the meditation and not trying to reach any particular result. Let your heart be your compass as you navigate the breathtaking waters of these ancient meditations.

Each of the heart meditations can be developed to the level of absorption concentration. Concentration meditation has three levels of concentration:

1 **Momentary:** It is happening just in this moment and then changes in the next moment.
2 **Access:** Deep sustaining concentration with little discomfort and many joyful experiences.
3 **Absorption:** The deepest concentration with no discomfort and immense joy and bliss. This level is also called *jhāna*, which is a nondual state with no subject or object or any sense of a "me" as you typically know yourself.

In absorption, there is no thinking, yet there is full awareness and an unwavering connection with the object of meditation. Absorption concentration is the spiritual potential of these heart meditations. It is not necessary to experience absorption concentration for these heart meditations to have a profound impact on your heart, your behavior, and your life.

Here is a brief introduction to the chapters' main components.

Resistances

For each meditation practice in this section, I reveal common resistances to the natural heart state that the meditation is opening. We all have resistances in our lives, and when we recognize and witness them, they come out of the shadows of our minds and into the light of truth. We do not want to invoke a spiritual bypass, going around what feels uncomfortable in order to maintain a spiritual self-image. We need to be with the truth of what is being experienced. Acceptance of what is actually happening is crucial support on a spiritual path.

Once you accept that you do indeed have a particular resistance, you can use the questions in each chapter to explore your history with it and relationship to it. While being close with one of the resistances, can you make contact with its energetic quality? Let's take anger as an example. It has a lot of raw strength in its energy. Can you feel anger's raw strength? If not, is there a block to your contact with that vigorous energy? Can you set aside any self-judgment relating to each resistance? To the extent possible, fully feel the energy of each resistance. Do not act out or outwardly express the particular resistance during the exercises, except in writing, if you'd like, in the space provided after the questions. This is meant to be internal processing only!

Similar Feelings

There are also similar emotions to the heart quality we are orienting toward. In each chapter in this section, there are exercises for distinguishing emotional affect from our true nature's heart.

Category of Beings

In each heart meditation exercise, there is a category-of-beings list. This is the traditional list that meditators use to express a particular heart quality. It is presented from easiest category to most challenging. This allows the meditator to develop that particular meditation while sharing it with those beings who will benefit. As the heart quality of the specific meditation becomes more accessible and stable, we can ultimately share it with those who regularly push our buttons. It is richly gratifying to discover your heart opening to someone for whom you frequently feel anger or hatred. I recommend that you work with a minimum of five people from each category of beings with each meditation. This will give you a deeper experience of that group, which will open your heart more fully to the people in that category.

Supportive Phrases

In the Buddha's Heart practices, supportive phrases assist our journey by helping our awareness stay with the meditative object, the focus of that particular meditation. When starting the meditation, we repeat this phrase silently within.

You may find that, as concentration deepens, it is not necessary to repeat the whole phrase to stay close to the meditative object. The phrase may even begin to feel burdensome. This is the time to shorten the phrase for meditative ease. Contact with your true nature's heart quality will support the meditation. I provide standard and suggested shortened phrases for each heart meditation. If you find that while using the shortened phrase you are unable to stay with the meditative object, return to the full supportive phrase.

4

Innate Goodness

INNATE GOODNESS IS an important meditation. It counteracts any beliefs we hold that we are not good enough or not lovable. By steeping in your innate goodness, you will feel better about yourself, feel more at ease, and meet your resistances with more tenderness. It is a meditation I practice regularly and suggest my senior students do, too. It infuses your consciousness with your goodness. This meditation results in feeling more present and more grounded in your life. It develops greater resiliency to be with your tender places.

Resistances to Innate Goodness

The resistances to innate goodness meditation are self-talk, self-judgments, and compulsive doing.

Self-Talk

Regrettably, many people today engage in a significant amount of negative self-talk. If we were to track our thoughts and self-referencing (i.e., how we refer to ourselves externally and internally), we would find a lot of negative inner talk. A portion of our self-talk is internalized criticism we received as youngsters. I suspect that due to our vulnerability and tendency to idealize and worship our early caregivers, we believe a great deal of what we were told. In addition, as we progress through school, we are given feedback and graded on our work. That too is information we receive directly as judgment. These judgments color the external self that we present to the world and the internal self we take ourselves to be.

What do you say to yourself when you are alone?

_____

_____

_____

How would you candidly describe yourself?

_____

How are you affected by your self-talk?

Self-Judgments

Self-judgments are due in part to the functioning of a mental structure known as the "inner critic" or the "super-ego." The superego was introduced to modern depth psychology by Sigmund Freud. He apportioned our mind into three parts: ego, id, and superego. In my understanding, the ego is the normal functioning of our personality. The id is the accumulation of all our survival instincts—our drive for food, shelter, sleep, and sex. The id is neither socialized nor polite; it wants what it wants and for the most part does not care how its wants are met. Like a supervisor, parent, or even an older sibling, the superego tries its best to rein in or control the id drives in an effort to make us appear more civilized and socially acceptable. But the problem is that it often makes us feel small, incompetent, and unlovable.

One of the effects of the near-constant presence of the superego is that we usually believe its negative judgments— that little voice saying, "You did this wrong," "You are so stupid," or "You make so many mistakes." When we believe the superego's statements about us, we develop a fairly negative internal sense of self and can be discouraged easily. This limits most aspects of our life, including our spiritual unfoldment. In walking the spiritual path, we need to develop—even cultivate—inner space and spaciousness. Spaciousness is needed for our deeper nature to arise in our consciousness. If spaciousness is crowded out by the negative criticisms of the superego, our spiritual practice will be slower to mature.

Working with the superego means being assertive and direct with it. When a superego judgment arises ("You did it wrong again!"), you must push back. With force, the spiritual student needs to say, "Back off," "Get lost," or "Go away!" You need to have the type of energy you would use if confronted by an aggressive dog. You do not want to escalate the confrontation, but you need to meet and stop the aggression of the superego. When you are too gentle with the superego, it is unfazed. When you confront the superego, you are challenging its judgment of you and clearing space internally.

With innate goodness meditation, we soften, tenderize, and open our heart to the beautiful qualities of our deeper nature. You may benefit from ongoing one-on-one work with a teacher skilled in engaging the superego while supporting spiritual unfoldment.

What is your history with self-judgments?

_____

_____

_____

What are your usual self-judgments?

_____

_____

_____

When do self-judgments typically arise for you?

_____

_____

_____

Compulsive Doing

No caregiver has the capacity to always be attuned to a child's needs. It is inevitable that caregivers sometimes become overwhelmed or distracted by life's demands. The result is that, as children, we do not feel our needs are fully met. We become convinced that we only receive food, love, clean clothes, and diapers because we smile or coo in a certain way that pleases our caregiver. This supports the belief that, in life, what we receive from others depends on what we are doing, rather than on simply being ourselves.

I was raised by an attentive and loving caregiver hired by my parents. She was sensitive to my needs and, for the most part, happy to meet them. My parents, in contrast, were distracted by their struggling relationship and the demands of my siblings. When my caregiver stopped working for my family, I began to believe that when I received attention, food, and shelter, it was in direct response to my doing something pleasing to my parents. I found that displaying intelligence, being funny, or being self-sufficient were behaviors my parents appreciated and rewarded. If I was unable to act as my parents expected, I would occasionally resort to negative behavior, which also generated attention—not satisfying attention, but it was still attention. My upbringing led to a pattern of compulsive doing. Does this sound familiar to you?

What is your history with compulsive doing?

_____

_____

_____

How do you seek attention at this stage
of life?

_____

_____

_____

Do you seek attention through positive or
negative behavior?

_____

_____

_____

What Can Appear Similar to Innate Goodness?

Egoic Behavior

We can confuse being with our innate goodness with egoic behavior. Egoic behavior is inviting others to see us as we desire to be seen—to witness and mirror our most cherished self-image. In this case, we seek for others to validate our sense of self—for example, confirming that we are kind and helpful. If they do not and instead, for example, communicate their opinion that our supposedly kind and helpful behavior is selfish and manipulative, we may feel negatively about ourselves and judgmental toward these other people.

> *With innate goodness, we do not have to do anything for the goodness to be in our consciousness and heart.*

With innate goodness, we do not have to *do* anything for the goodness to be in our consciousness and heart. We cease seeking any particular reflection from others. It is simply being, without doing, that exposes the goodness. We have less concern about how we are seen. Innate goodness gives us more balance, natural confidence, and self-love.

What is your history with egoic behavior?

_____

_____

_____

How does egoic behavior show up for you?

_____

_____

_____

Why does egoic behavior arise for you?

_____

_____

_____

Innate Goodness Practice

This meditation encourages you to be with your inherent, unconditioned goodness, which is not dependent on you being any particular way or behaving in a prescribed manner. It is not a goodness that comes from being a student who gets high grades, a valued employee, or even a helpful person. It is your goodness that emanates from your Beingness. Remember a time when you were with a young puppy or a newborn baby. Holding them, you can see the value, the beauty, the goodness they emanate without *doing* anything. This is the goodness we want to make contact with and cultivate in the meditation.

One reason we cultivate innate goodness is as a cultivation of self-love. Love is a powerful heart quality. It can soften the rough edges of our self-image and bolster our sense of contentment while supporting deep inner exploration. Love is essential to our inner unfoldment and to deepening our access to the mysterious properties of the Absolute realm.

In the innate goodness meditation, there is no category of beings as we are doing it solely for ourselves. There are no support phrases for this meditation.

> Seat yourself in a comfortable seat, either on a meditation cushion or on a comfortable chair.
> Sit upright, with your spine straight while maintaining the natural S curve of the spine.
> Try to have your hips higher than your legs.
> Feel your balance and posture.
> Place your hands high on your lap or thighs to avoid straining your neck.
> Take a number of slow, deep belly breaths.
> Relax your body.
> Rest your awareness in your heart center.
> Maintaining your awareness in your heart center, picture yourself at a time in your life when you can connect with your innate goodness. For some people, they can see this in their current image. For others, innate goodness is easier to see at a younger age.
> Take the time to find a picture of yourself when you have direct contact with your innate goodness.

> Continue the meditation by taking relaxed, deep belly breaths, relaxing, feeling/sensing your heart center.

> Let goodness radiate in your heart center.

> Use your breath to draw the innate goodness closer to your heart center.

> After a suitable time with a feeling of stability, try to let go of any mental image of yourself that you are using as support for the meditation.

> When you can let go of your mental picture, stay with the goodness itself. Continue to breathe goodness into your heart center.

> Let the goodness radiate fully within your consciousness.

> Accept its presence, letting it affect you as it will.

This is a meditation that can be done at the start of your regular meditation period, or it can be the sole focus of the session. You can practice this away from the meditation cushion or chair when waiting in line at the store, bank, or office, by taking a moment to do some belly breaths and opening your awareness to your innate goodness. Let it collect and radiate in your heart center and soothe your consciousness wherever you may be.

Love is a powerful heart quality. It can soften the rough edges of our self-image and bolster our sense of contentment while supporting deep inner exploration. Love is essential to our inner unfoldment and to deepening our access to the mysterious properties of the Absolute realm.

5

Upekkhā: *Equanimity*

WHEN WE ARE out of balance psychologically, our instinct is to smooth the choppy waves of our personality by reaffirming our sense of self. We try to find others to mirror our personality patterning—by seeing us as kind and generous, for example—because when we feel witnessed, our personality compulsions can temporarily relax. Yet this only gives us the illusion of stability. Our personality patterning is just a reflection—a mentally constructed imitation—of our deeper nature. Feeling internally imbalanced prevents us from seeing more deeply into our behavior and feeling the inner perception of lack. We focus upon and get ensnared by the surface issues in life. By habit and social conditioning, we prioritize what is fundamentally false over what is most true, our Beingness—the Presence of the Absolute.

Equanimity is a feeling of perfect balance. Everything that is occurring inside or outside of us is exactly right in this moment. Equanimity generates a quality of trust in our hearts that we are exactly in the right place at the right time. It empowers us to possess a level of acceptance, of balanced perspective, for the objective, universal truth that is always here with us. We open our awareness, our consciousness, to equanimity as a manifestation of the Absolute by orienting toward ultimate reality, unadorned truth.

> *Equanimity generates a quality of trust in our hearts that we are exactly in the right place at the right time.*

Before learning the practice of equanimity, we will look at the psychological resistances to it.

Resistances to *Upekkhā*

There are natural, mostly psychological, resistances to equanimity and its harmonious quality. These are resentment, greed, and anxiety about the uncontrollability of life.

Resentment

Resentment is an angry, even bitter, rejecting of the present moment when we feel we have been treated unfairly. There is an internal conclusion that what is occurring is unwelcome. Typically, we reject events that do not reflect our sense of self in the world. This rejection is fueled when we are not seen as our cherished self-image. When this occurs, we respond to what is happening with an angry rejection of reality.

What is your history with resentment?

_____

_____

How does resentment show up for you?

_____

_____

Why does resentment arise for you?

_____

_____

_____

Greed

Greed is an unquenchable thirst for more. It is a yearning that compulsively reaches for whatever we think will make us whole, happy, and complete. It is a thirst for greater admiration, increased recognition, and more possessions to try to fill our neediness. This greed comes from our firm belief in our self-deficiency.

What is your history with greed?

_____

_____

_____

How does greed show up for you?

_____

_____

_____

Why does greed arise for you?

_____

_____

_____

Anxiety about the Uncontrollability of Life

From our earliest years, we try to direct life in a desperate strategy to be witnessed and cherished. We know how we want to be seen. Regrettably, life unfolds as it will, and we are often disappointed by it and the realization that we ultimately have little to no control. This exposure of our inner lack leads us to develop anxiousness.

What is your history with anxiety about the uncontrollability of life?

_____

_____

_____

How does anxiety about the
uncontrollability of life show up for you?

_____

_____

_____

Why does anxiety about the
uncontrollability of life arise for you?

_____

_____

_____

These resistances to harmony and equanimity prevent objective truth from fully being perceived. Using misdirection and suppression, we desperately try to influence life's outcomes to confirm to others our most prized self, even though we know from experience that our best strategies will be unsuccessful.

Yet, being on a spiritual path means we dedicate our lives to truth. Not necessarily the truth that supports our sense of self but rather ultimate, objective, universal truth. This path of truth can be uncomfortable, too, but there is satisfaction in being with the truth even when it is painful.

What Can Appear Similar to Equanimity?

Indifference

Indifference is a psychological numbing to anticipated pain, suffering, or dissatisfaction with life. We want everyone in our life to be impressed by our most polished sense of self. Yet we must reconcile ourselves to experiencing repeated disappointment, which leads to a surrender of not caring. Indifference is a strategy we use to block the pain of life's lack of value for who we are. If we numb ourselves, we believe we are protected from any misattunement with others.

One crucial difference between indifference and equanimity is acceptance. With equanimity, there is a deep acceptance of what is happening and there is minimal effort to control an outcome. Equanimity and indifference also feel distinct; indifference is a suppressing of your vitality, while with equanimity there is an open, warm felt sense of a rightness about life as it is unfolding.

What is your history with indifference?

_____

_____

_____

How does indifference show up for you?

_____

_____

_____

Why does indifference arise for you?

_____

_____

_____

Upekkhā *Practice*

The meditative object in *upekkhā* meditation is truth, seeing phenomena as it actually is.

Category of Beings

With each heart meditation, there is a sequence of beings. These are the people for whom we practice *upekkhā*, progressing from easiest to hardest.

> Neutral person
> Benefactor
> Friend
> Difficult person
> Self
> All beings

We start with a neutral person because it is easier to accept and see the truth for that person than for someone with whom we are extensively intertwined. Note that we do not start with ourselves. This is due to the truism that we are not the easiest being in which to witness the movement of objective truth, ultimate reality. This is due to our historic pattern of acting as our own strident advocate and promoter— a pattern we are questioning with the Buddha's

Heart practices. As a reminder, I suggest committing to a minimum of five specific people from each category of being with each meditation.

Supportive Phrase: "All beings are heir to their karma."

> Begin with a number of slow, steady, deep belly breaths.

> Starting with the neutral person, try to either picture them in your mind's eye or feel them in your heart energy.

> As you come to retain an image or felt sense of that person, silently repeat the supporting phrase, "All beings are heir to their karma." (I use the term "karma" to mean the universal law of cause and effect.)

> Continue deep, open, relaxed breathing. No force is needed.

> Maintain the felt sense or image of this neutral person. Silently repeat the supporting phrase, "All beings are heir to their karma." Open your heart and mind to feel deeply, to be impacted.

> Stay focused on this neutral person. When you find your awareness has wandered away from

> the truth of this neutral person, gently return it without judgment or self-criticism.
>
>) When you find that you have deeply understood the truth of at least five neutral people from their perspective, you can continue on to the next group in the category of beings.

Equanimity cultivates an evenness, a smoothness, when we witness life events unfolding. When equanimity is present, we respond to life with greater ease and deeper acceptance. We feel less resistance and recognize that we are a part of the flowing stream of life.

On the two-month retreat I did with my teacher, the Venerable Pa Auk Sayadaw, I engaged with this practice at a very deep level. After one multihour *upekkhā* meditation period, I went on a hike. I saw a large tree that had recently fallen. It had massive roots that had upended the surrounding hillside, with fresh dirt splayed around. I could see there was a nest in the upper branches of the tree. The nest had been slightly crushed in the fall. Although I could not see any injured animals, I felt the equanimity of nature. There was a profound neutrality present. There was no intention to harm the nest or the animals living there. It was simply a matter of natural conditions reaching a point where the tree toppled under its own weight and angled position. This was a powerful learning for me. I recognized I had attributed some form of intent to nature. I held a view that there was a balancing underway in life that was sometimes helpful, even generous, and other times harmful, even tragic. I was adding a mental meaning to something that was unplanned in nature. It was just what happened.

When you conclude with all categories of beings, it is time to undertake the next heart meditation—*mudita*, translated as "empathetic joy."

6

Mudita: *Empathetic Joy*

WE HAVE LEARNED TO SEE ourselves as separate from other people. From the understanding of our deeper nature, this view is incorrect. We are like waves, all of the same ocean. Most people have a limited ability to consistently know the undivided wholeness of our deeper nature. While we are rooted in our separateness, we are more isolated and distant from others' joy and pain. This self-isolation can develop an inner numbness, a walling off of our sensitivity, openness, and receptivity toward others. We have difficulty perceiving the Oneness in another, and we identify chiefly with our personal needs and wants.

From this solitary view, we believe that there is a finite amount of love, food, and emotional tenderness. Psychologically, we believe recognition and praise are in short supply, and if someone else gets this positive attention before we do, we are convinced that we have lost. Consequently, we covet and hoard everything of value, from attention to food. We may feel our survival depends upon being seen. This invites competition, not cooperation.

> *In truth, when one of us receives a benefit or recognition, we all benefit. The Oneness is enriched when good things happen to anyone. It is as though we are all in a shared pond. When the water rises in one portion of the pond, it soon rises in all other areas.*

Muditā (empathetic joy) arises in our heart when there is no perceived separation between living beings, when we know the true fabric of reality is a unified Oneness. In truth, when one of us receives a benefit or recognition, we all benefit. The Oneness is enriched when good things happen to anyone. It is as though we are all in a shared pond. When the water rises in one portion of the pond, it soon rises in all other areas.

When we are not abiding in this field of Oneness, we will be subject to one or more of the resistances to *muditā*.

Resistances to *Mudita*

The resistances to *mudita* are envy and jealousy.

Envy

Envy arises when we ache to have another's success or good fortune be ours. The other's success feels like our failure. Envy feels like a loss. In envy, we sadly witness another person receiving something that we want. This ache can cause us to feel we will never get what we need. Envy is not just craving someone else's success; it stirs our conviction of our future losses.

What is your history with envy?

_____

_____

_____

Under what circumstances does envy arise in your life?

_____

_____

Why does envy persist in arising for you?

Jealousy

Witnessing another's joy and success can feel like our wound. We not only want what they have; we also feel anger when they receive it.

Part of what can drive jealousy is a childhood history of abandonment or misattunement by our early caregivers. If we felt that a caregiver or parent gave more love, affection, or attention to a peer or sibling, there will be an inner conviction in our unquenchable neediness. When another gets the attention we are seeking, it can trigger the anger of jealousy. We all desire to be seen and treated as uniquely special. When we are in contact with our deeper nature, we know that there is enough for all. We can celebrate another's good fortune as if it is our own.

What is your history with jealousy?

_____

_____

_____

How do you see jealousy arise in your life?

_____

_____

_____

Why does jealousy arise for you?

_____

_____

_____

What Can Appear Similar to Empathetic Joy?

Comparing

Comparing will only occur when we are landed in the isolation of our personality patterning. We will exclusively see our own needs and wants. Our perception will not extend further than getting what we crave, what we feel is crucial to our very survival.

When we compare ourselves to another, we reside in our core lacking, the insufficiencies in our deficient emptiness. We will feel unlovable, not good enough—a failure. From this familiar feeling of deficiency, we will be disconnected from our hearts and unable to feel the Oneness of reality, the open generosity or *mudita* for another.

What is your history with comparing?

_____

_____

_____

How does comparing arise in your life?

_____

_____

Why does comparing arise for you?

Insincerity in Our Good Wishes

We may feel a certain internal or external pressure to celebrate another's good fortune. Yet if our heart is closed and we feel our own longing and neediness instead of our sufficiency, there will be a cloying, sticky quality to our offered words of congratulations. We are diminishing our relationship with the other person through unintended insincerity.

What is your history with being insincere in offering good wishes?

How does being insincere with good wishes show up for you?

_____

_____

_____

Why does being insincere with good wishes arise for you?

_____

_____

_____

Grasping for the Pleasant

Typically, we highly value pleasant experiences. We may use planning to avoid what is either neutral or unpleasant. We might view pleasant experiences as a measure of our goodness, our success. If we have an experience that does not meet this ideal of our goodness, it is disappointing. Rather than being open to all experiences, we filter life experiences

exclusively for what feels good or makes us happy. All other
experiences are rejected as not being what we deserve.

What is your history with grasping for the pleasant?

_____

_____

_____

How does grasping for the pleasant show up for you?

_____

_____

_____

Why does grasping for the pleasant arise for you?

_____

_____

_____

Mudita *Practice*

The meditative object in *mudita* meditation is another's happiness or their good fortune.

Category of Beings

> Friend (whom it is easy to feel happy for)
> Benefactor
> Neutral person
> Difficult person
> All beings

Supportive Phrase: "May you continue to be happy and content."

Mudita is never undertaken for ourselves. We use gratitude practice to clarify and deepen our own happiness and joy. It is helpful to commence *mudita* practice for a friend or person with whom we are close. Feeling empathetic joy for a dear friend will be easier than doing so for someone we do not know well.

Silently repeat the supportive phrase to assist you in staying close to your friend in your mind's eye.

Once we have completed our *muditā* practice for a few friends, we next move on to doing *muditā* for a benefactor. This can be a trusted teacher or another mentoring person. This benefactor will also be a person for whom feeling *muditā* will be relatively easy.

The next category of being we turn to after doing *muditā* for a few benefactors is the neutral person. Selecting the neutral person can be a little more challenging. With practice, you will find feeling *muditā* for the store clerk, bank teller, or mail person is effortless.

The difficult person is next in our category of beings. Locating the difficult person's joy may take diligence. You may find that you cannot feel *muditā* for the whole of the difficult person's life but may find it for just an area of their life. When I first did this practice, I was struggling with feeling *muditā* for a difficult person. I saw that in my struggle I was looking at their entire life, including the objectionable places. Yet by staying with the *muditā* meditation, I came to see that I did appreciate their tenderness and dedicated love for their family. By focusing on that person's love of family, I was able to offer *mudita* for that difficult person.

The *mudita* meditation practice can be challenging when first undertaken. Part of the initial challenge of *mudita* is experiencing our resistances to it. It is useful to know that the resistances are common. With sustained *mudita* practice, the tender subtlety and the warm glow of empathetic joy will enliven your awareness, open your heart, and positively impact your relationships. Developing a *mudita* meditation practice will allow you to be more wholehearted when relating to others. When a friend has a life success, it will not automatically trigger a comparison, a reminder of what is lacking. Rather we will openheartedly rejoice with our friend when *mudita* is present.

I grew up in a larger family. It was common for one of my siblings to have a life success or receive something special from a parent. It was just the functioning of the law of averages. Yet often when a sibling had a success, I compared myself to them, felt a lack, and then resented them and their success. I found this empathetic joy practice to be an amazing, life-changing learning experience. I not only felt more deeply connected to others, but I could be genuinely happy for them without engaging in any comparing or self-judging. Through this practice, the quality of my life improved because I was suffering less!

7

Karuṇā: *Compassion*

ON OUR JOURNEY of spiritual awakening and embodiment, we will pass through many familiar areas of our history, memories, and psyche that remain painful. Yet the light of objective, universal truth beckons us closer to our tender places. Navigating these difficult areas, we need to have tenderness and compassion for ourselves.

Compassion is often misapplied in Buddhist practice. Many Buddhists believe that the function of compassion is to *take away* painful life events. This is not compassion's full benefit. Using compassion in our meditative practices provides gentle support, a *kindhearted holding* that allows us, and others, to be with our pain and persevere.

Compassion helps us draw closer to an enduring truth that is very different from the subjective truth that supports the story of our lives. In our life narratives, we cast ourselves in a particular role, typically that of the pure, good, innocent one. With sustained *karuṇā* practice, we begin to see that we maintain this young, pure, innocent self-image to present others as the source of our pain, and we are confronted by the universal truth that we encompass many emotions and levels of identity.

Compassion assists us in developing the ability to be with whatever state of mind or emotion is present. When we are not exclusively seeking good experiences and instead feel what is authentically present, it draws us closer to the truth of our Beingness.

Compassion assists us in developing the ability to be with *whatever* state of mind or emotion is present. When we are not exclusively seeking good experiences and instead feel what is authentically present, it draws us closer to the truth of our Beingness.

Resistances to *Karuṇā*

The typical resistances to *karuṇā* are enjoyment of another's suffering and cruelty.

Enjoyment of Another's Suffering

Adults live a life mixed with uplifting joy and profound disappointment. We have been hurt and hurt others. This leaves us as a mixture of maturity and immaturity. At times we are kind and accommodating to another's behavior. On other occasions we will be instantly hurt, angry, or reactive.

By adulthood, we are committed to our social and political opinions and beliefs. We hold many of these opinions as indisputable truths. Whenever you hold something to be an indisputable truth, it will be difficult to question that belief.

Usually when another person holds a contrary opinion to ours, we see the other person as alien to us and we turn away in rejection. This is common specifically with differing political or religious opinions.

Should this contrary person encounter life difficulties, we may feel their suffering is justified for their abhorrent opinions, and we may take a secret delight in their pain. This is enjoyment of another's suffering.

What is your history with enjoying another's suffering?

_____

_____

_____

How does enjoying another's suffering show up for you?

_____

_____

_____

Why does enjoying another's suffering arise for you?

_____

_____

_____

Cruelty

To fully engage the path of awakening and functioning self-realization, we must—I repeat, *must*—be able to be with all aspects and expressions of our psychology. We will not progress to the deeper, more realized experiences unless we can wade into what feels like our personal swamp, our rejected and disowned parts, when present.

You may have an early memory of taking quiet, secret delight in another's suffering. It may have been someone who previously hurt you. Perhaps after they hurt you, you witnessed them undergo something painful. Maybe you felt a little glee seeing this. Maybe you even said something that added to their suffering. Intentionally making another's suffering worse is cruelty.

When you take pleasure in the suffering of a person you dislike or hate, you are suspending the spontaneous arising of compassion. We need to honestly and courageously wade into the discomfort of our past hurtful behaviors to be fully open to compassion. As we learn to reveal and recognize our cruelty, we are less unconsciously run by it. Cruelty can then become a choice, rather than an unconscious behavior. Once cruelty becomes an express choice, it can also be abandoned. This turning from cruelty helps us open to the presence of gentle compassion.

What is your history with cruelty or being cruel?

_____

_____

_____

How does cruelty show up for you?

_____

_____

_____

Why does cruelty arise for you?

_____

_____

_____

What Can Appear Similar to Compassion?

We might mistake pity, righteous anger, or fear for compassion.

Pity

When we pity someone, we are observing them with superiority. We are witnessing their suffering from an emotionally elevated distance. We may feel bad for them, yet we cannot offer authentic support when we are anchored in pity. We see the person we pity as a victim. We almost believe they might deserve this suffering. Pity is not supportive or kind but judgmental and often condescending.

What is your history with pity?

_____

_____

_____

How does pity show up for you?

_____

_____

_____

Why does pity arise for you?

_____

_____

_____

Righteous Anger

Righteous anger also originates from an inner superiority. It feels unquestionably right. We *know* what is best for everyone. When another does not behave or act in the way we think is best, it can trigger our anger. The anger stirs our righteousness, resulting in our lashing out. Our righteous anger on behalf of someone who is suffering is not compassion. We are not offering support that helps the hurting person be with their pain. Instead, in righteous anger we may be attacking the cause of the pain.

What is your history with righteous anger?

_____

_____

How does righteous anger show up for you?

_____

_____

_____

Why does righteous anger arise for you?

_____

_____

_____

Fear

Fear arises when we are feeling disconnected from our heart. When our heart is hidden to us, we feel abandoned, hopeless, or helpless. In reacting with fear, we are contracting into ourselves; we are neither meeting what is occurring nor seeking a healthy response. We withdraw to escape. If we feel fearful witnessing another's pain, we pull within and shut down instead of offering them compassion or helpful support.

What is your history with fear?

_____

_____

_____

How does fear show up for you?

_____

_____

_____

Why does fear arise for you?

_____

_____

_____

Karuṇā *Practice*

The meditative object in *karuṇā* meditation is someone's suffering. We are being present to—witnessing—another's pain and suffering. Ideally, we will simultaneously be with our own reaction to another's suffering and offer them kindness, trust, and compassionate holding.

Category of Beings

> Suffering person

> Self

> Benefactor

> Friend

> Neutral person

> Difficult person

> All beings

Supportive Phrase: "May you be free from suffering."

When undertaking *karuṇā* meditation, silently repeat the supportive phrase to assist you in holding the suffering person in your mind's eye.

We start *karuṇā* meditation holding, in our mind's eye, a suffering person we know. We hold this person while maintaining awareness of their suffering. Sometimes we can feel the cause of their suffering. You do not need to know or be with the source of their suffering to participate in *karuṇā* meditation. Sometimes the person suffering is unknowingly causing their own suffering.

When you have a clear image or felt sense of the suffering person, feel their suffering. Do not try to find fixes for them. Compassion is being with their suffering, not resolving it or taking away their pain.

Take deep belly breaths and be with their pain. When your meditative concentration develops to a sufficient depth, you will feel a tender kindness or an inclusive holding arise in response to the other's pain.

Stay with the category of suffering person until each time you picture a suffering person, your heart opens and you feel kind support and tenderness arising spontaneously. When you can be with their suffering without feeling the impulse to fix it, you will likely feel mental clarity.

Compassion meditation practice helps us to be more sensitive, more transparently open. By being in direct contact with open caring and supportive tenderness, we can be genuinely present to another.

One common response to another's suffering is to offer a fix. For many years, this was my automatic response to another's suffering. I did not spend much time witnessing their struggles. I quickly moved past their pain to find a fix. I could see then, and even more clearly now, that by not honoring their struggle, I was minimizing their difficulty and adding to their suffering. My approach left them feeling unseen while I contributed to their pain. Although adding to their suffering was not my intent, it was the result of my inability to witness and feel my own suffering. *Karuṇā* practice has softened me sufficiently to be willing to be directly and authentically with my own pain and suffering. When we can do this, and as we gain more experience being present to another's suffering, we can meet their suffering with compassion. We can appreciate them for who they are, honor the struggles life has directed to them, and hold the best wishes for them. The ability to offer another being unconditional love is developed through the meditative practice of *mettā* (loving-kindness).

8

Mettā: *Loving-Kindness*

HUMAN LIFE CAN BE really painful and difficult. Our well-intentioned caregivers did their best to support our times of struggle when we were infants. They taught, and modeled, many ways to avoid life's challenges.

> *If we are truly on a path of opening to our deeper nature and unfolding self-realization, we must directly meet the truth of life's pains and pleasures. We cannot exclusively seek pleasant experiences if we are to walk a true path of liberation.*

We will never be able to control, or deflect, painful life experiences. It is a core understanding in Buddhism that life contains unsatisfactoriness. If we are truly on a path of opening to our deeper nature and unfolding self-realization, we must directly meet the truth of life's pains and pleasures. We cannot exclusively seek pleasant experiences if we are to walk a true path of liberation.

Mettā meditation provides a way to meet the challenges of painful life experiences with openhearted love. *Mettā* is usually translated as "loving-kindness." Feeling into loving and kindness, we sense a particular support, an enduring lightness that is inherent. This is the loving lightness we need to meet life's challenges and struggles with an open heart.

Resistances to *Mettā*

For *mettā* meditation, there are a number of well-known resistances: hatred, anger, aversion, self-hatred, self-judgment, and guilt.

Hatred

Having a deeper understanding of hatred will permit us to more fully contact loving-kindness. Hatred is often coupled with a feeling of powerlessness. As children, we felt adults held power over us. We felt small, perhaps insignificant, helpless, and even hopeless, and we had limited options for how we could interact with the adults. We were afraid the nurturing and support we did receive would diminish if we fully expressed our dissatisfaction. One of the ways we could internally support ourselves to silently, internally fight back was to seethe with hatred. Feeling hatred as young children, we could imagine slaying the powerful adults. This is not a mature response to feeling overwhelmed by another's power, yet hatred could buttress our aching heart. Hatred can be understood as a desperate strategy our wounded self adopts in order to feel it can survive a devastating verbal or emotional attack. It is critical to our spiritual unfolding that we be able to acknowledge and experience our inner hatred. Unless we can be with our hatred as it arises, we will not fully feel the delicate lightness of warmhearted loving-kindness, or *mettā*.

What is your history with hatred?

_____

_____

_____

How does hatred show up for you?

_____

_____

_____

Why does hatred arise for you?

_____

_____

_____

Anger

Anger is a more moderated response to feeling attacked than hatred is. Anger is a needed emotion. By this, I mean it is an emotional reaction that we need to feel when it arises. I am not advocating outwardly expressing anger anytime it arises. Rather, I am encouraging you to fully feel your anger when it is authentically present. It does not need to be acted upon or expressed for us to be with it. Anger is not to be rejected or suppressed. When we suppress emotions, they smolder until finally erupting, usually inappropriately. We also do not want to be preoccupied with our anger. We want to allow it to appear and disappear naturally, without our influence. Suppressing or dwelling in our anger will numb us to fully contacting the delicate loving-kindness of *mettā*.

What is your history with anger?

_____

_____

_____

How does anger show up for you?

_____

_____

_____

Why does anger arise for you?

_____

_____

_____

Aversion

When we meet unwanted, painful experiences, one popular response is aversion. Aversion is a sweeping rejection of what is happening now, and it allows us to avoid or hide from reality. The rationale behind this is that when we can suppress the pain of life, we will only have pleasant, pleasurable experiences. But this does not work. We are only temporarily masking the emotional suffering, and it will probably still be here after our aversion wanes. If we commit to aversion as an avoidant life strategy, we unknowingly narrow our connection with our heart. Aversion strategies only serve to wall off our hearts and to limit our contact with and impressionability to the warm, melting tenderness of loving-kindness.

What is your history with aversion?

_____

_____

_____

How does aversion show up for you?

_____

_____

Why does aversion arise for you?

_____

_____

_____

Self-Hatred and Self-Judgment

Each of us has internalized our early caregivers' criticism of us. As children, our very survival can feel dependent upon agreeing with the criticism of us. We may see our caregiver as perfect and feel we are deeply flawed in comparison. Sometimes we join in their negative judgment of us to temper the sting of their rejection. If we keep up this behavior long enough, it becomes an unchallenged belief, despite the suffering we feel. If we accept their criticism, it can smolder into ongoing, unconscious self-criticism, even self-hatred. When we are enmeshed in self-hatred or self-judgment, we close our connection to our heart. We are not welcoming the openheartedness needed for the arising of loving-kindness.

What is your history with self-hatred and
self-judgment?

_____

_____

_____

How does self-hatred and self-judgment
show up for you?

_____

_____

_____

Why does self-hatred and self-judgment
arise for you?

_____

_____

_____

Guilt

On our spiritual journey, from First Awakening to fully integrated self-realization, we must be oriented inward. We must become intimate with, and adept at navigating, our interiority of experience. This inner turn can feel disquieting. It can feel like we are rejecting our life, our loves, and our world, and abandoning our humanness. In effect, we are temporarily doing just that. Yet this necessary turning away is actually not a rejection of exterior life. Remarkably, as we turn inward, we come into greater contact and connection with the exterior world. When I went through this process, I realized that the more I turned inward, the more engaged and connected I felt with the outside world. My life made more sense as I was more authentic in my actions and behavior.

However, we may have accompanying feelings of unease, even guilt. The experience of happiness or gratification can trigger guilt that others are not able to enjoy these same pleasures. We may feel selfish or self-centered taking care of ourselves and not attending to the many issues of the world. When the guilt couples with the witnessing of another's suffering, it does not afford us sufficient interior space for loving-kindness to arise. We need to recognize, and be present to, our guilt as it arises. Guilt moves from unconscious to conscious under observation. The act of seeing it reduces its effect on us. Guilt, when witnessed, can become something we can engage with rather than something that overwhelms us.

What is your history with guilt?

_____

_____

_____

How does guilt show up for you?

_____

_____

_____

Why does guilt arise for you?

_____

_____

_____

What Can Appear Similar to Loving-Kindness?

There are a few emotional and psychological qualities we can mistake for loving-kindness. These are attachment, desire, and possessive love.

Attachment

Developing and inviting loving-kindness toward another is a light, open, unencumbered connection. It is generous of heart and free of any clinging or egoic stickiness. When the warmheartedness of loving-kindness is filtered through our personality patterning and our places of hurt, it may reveal our underlying neediness. This neediness confirms we are wanting recognition, validation, or appreciation from another to feel good about ourselves. Dependent attachment prevents us from being independent and self-sustaining.

What is your history with attachment?

_____

_____

_____

How does attachment show up for you?

_____

_____

_____

Why does attachment arise for you?

_____

_____

_____

Desire

Desire can be experienced as an emotional longing. It can be wanting another person to see us in a particular way. It is also wanting material possessions to support us to feel full and complete. We typically seek recognition, appreciation, or value. Desire is wanting whatever we feel we lack. What we psychologically desire is intended to fill our sense of inner lacking, which is the unexamined territories of our personality patterning and the felt disconnection with the Presence of the Absolute.

What is your history with desire?

_____

_____

_____

How does desire show up for you?

_____

_____

_____

Why does desire arise for you?

_____

_____

_____

Possessive Love

Possessive love is an insistent demand that another person prioritize satisfying our neediness and heart's hunger over ministering to themselves. We do not wish to share the object of our love with anyone else. This is an unhealthy love, and we will ultimately lash out in hurt and anger when our love interest is not solely attending to us.

What is your history with possessive love?

_____

_____

_____

How does possessive love show up for you?

_____

_____

_____

Why does possessive love arise for you?

_____

_____

_____

Emotional neediness lacks the stability and freedom of loving-kindness. By "freedom," I mean that the love is freely given without consideration of any return. It is open, spacious, and unrestricted.

Mettā *Practice*

Begin the *mettā* practice in your usual meditation posture and position. Taking deep belly breaths, let your awareness settle in your heart region.

Category of Beings

> Self
> Benefactor
> Friend
> Neutral person
> Difficult person
> All beings

Supportive Phrases: "May I be safe. May I be healthy. May I be happy. May I live with ease. May I be liberated."

Bring the image or felt sense of yourself to your mind's eye. It is best to select a time of your life when you can easily make contact with your innate goodness. For some people, this will be a picture of how you are today. For others, it will be easier picturing yourself at a younger age, even as an infant.

Lightly holding this image or felt sense of yourself, breathe into your heart area. Feel and sense your innate goodness. Innate goodness is not conditional on your behaving any certain way. It is the goodness that you radiate when relaxed, by simply being who you are.

Silently repeat the supportive phrases to assist you in staying with the felt sense or visual image of yourself in your mind's eye. As your meditation deepens and settles, it will become helpful to synthesize the phrases into a more condensed form. You can try to narrow the phrases to saying, "Safe, healthy, happy, ease, liberated."

Some people may have some layering, a numbing around their heart, and it may be challenging to feel their own innate goodness initially. Fortunately, this is a temporary barrier. If you feel blocked, try switching the meditative object from yourself to a benefactor. Once you spend time filling your heart area with innate goodness for a benefactor, it will be easier to access this quality of heart for yourself.

Go slowly.

Feel the innate goodness, your innate goodness, in your heart area.

Take the time to allow the goodness in your heart area to collect. This may take hours or days, even on retreat. It is important to follow the practice to be complete of heart. This fullness of *mettā* will be reached when it feels as though your heart area is overflowing with loving-kindness. This will be confirmed when you are off the meditation cushion or chair and engaged in life and you find that *mettā* is naturally, unintentionally flowing from your heart center toward others.

This is when you switch to the benefactor, the next being in the category of beings. Follow the same process, holding the benefactor in your mind's eye and feeling or seeing their innate goodness in your heart area.

Loving-kindness practice tenderizes our heart. The places in our heart where we have felt wounded by others can feel hard, stiff, distant. By feeling another's goodness and wishing them loving-kindness, we are removing the inner barriers that limit our heartful connection with another.

I first started loving-kindness meditation in the 1990s. I was in my thirties, early in my career as a lawyer, and attempting, unsuccessfully, to block off my heart to the pain of legal confrontation that was a part of the profession. In effect, I was trying to close my heart and wall off my feelings of tenderness to be more successful. As you may expect, this did not work. Not only was I still feeling the discomfort and pain of argumentative confrontation that was inherent in litigation, I was hardening my heart qualities to myself. This left me with fewer internal resources and did nothing to lessen my suffering.

As I began to practice loving-kindness meditation, I could feel a soft opening starting in my heart. It was not a weakness, as I expected, but a heart resiliency. In effect, I was gaining more dimension, more heart capacity, as well as the ability to be more present in my work, to take challenging interactions less personally, and to see that functioning as a lawyer did not require me to hide or mask my tenderness.

Heart
Purifying

THE FOLLOWING THREE MEDITATIONS are not tradition-
ally part of the *brahmavihāras*, the Buddha's Heart meditations.
Yet I have found them to be invaluable and indispensable in
my own meditative practice, and many of my students agree.

Regularly engaging in the acknowledgment of the gifts in
our lives through a gratitude practice, as outlined in Chapter
9, is powerful. Instead of focusing on what is lacking in us and
in our lives, we are turning toward the fruitfulness of life. We
are orienting to what is being offered to us.

As humans, we internally hold a lot of anger, resentment,
guilt, and shame. Much of this stems from unsatisfying
encounters and challenging interactions with others. We can
carry these feelings, in part, due to memories of unresolved
difficulties with others as well as judgments about our past
behavior. By engaging in a forgiveness practice, explored in
Chapter 10, we can intentionally, specifically recognize harmful behavior, possibly identify its causes, and form the inten-

tion to let go, to release the hurt we are holding. This releasing of old, emotionally charged memories and pain affords us internal open spaciousness. With open spaciousness, we can welcome deeper contact with our true nature as our path of awakening continues to unfold.

Part of the underlying reason we, as a species, orient toward the negative is the loss of contact with our deeper nature. This loss of contact with the Presence of the Absolute, which is our deeper nature, leads us to adopt a psychologically defensive view. We prioritize and seek what's missing or lacking in our lives. We monitor those around us to see which friend or family member is seeing us as we believe we should be seen. We want them to mirror our best self-image. We have temporarily lost our connection to our deeper nature, which results in uncertainty and worry.

The Oneness of Reality practices in Chapter 11 can support our reorienting toward our deepest truth: that we are a unique expression of the undivided wholeness of Presence. Turning toward and ultimately returning to this awake, aware Presence, and witnessing Presence as our true substance, brings our very being into a clearer focus. Through this undivided wholeness, we learn and understand how connected we always are to every other living being. In this place of undivided wholeness, when we breathe we feel and know the Earth and all its inhabitants are breathing, too.

9

Gratitude

BEING IN CONTACT with our gratitude is an important part of the heart's journey of awakening. When we are not in touch with our gratitude, there can be a slight hardening of the heart that is displayed through callousness and trivializing what we have been offered. By minimizing gratitude, we treat life's gifts dismissively and choose to believe they're solely the product of our actions.

> *Gratitude is a confirmation that we are part of an undivided wholeness that is abundant, full of generosity and love.*

Gratitude is an appreciation of what life offers us. Gratitude is a confirmation that we are part of an undivided wholeness that is abundant, full of generosity and love. There is truly no shortage of what we need to be sustained in our life and on our journey on the path of awakening. In this practice, we will make contact with all the people and material gifts life has afforded us. This contact helps us feel our authenticity of heart.

When I was a young Buddhist meditator, I was quite emotionally immature. I was convinced that progression in my meditative experience and awakenings was solely tied to my effort and willpower. I felt it was my effort alone that controlled my spiritual destiny. It took years—and kind teachers—for me to learn I was neither in control nor completely independent. This was a wake-up call for me that came about as my marriage was breaking down and family members were struggling with illness and death. There was literally nothing I could do, no action I could take, that could fix another's illness or death.

This is when I found a gratitude practice. As I named one person or quality in my life for which I was grateful, my heart was lightened. The heaviness of trying to control my life had become crushing to my soul-consciousness. Gratitude practice also led me to value the people in my life who were wholesome and unselfishly supportive of me.

We can feel gratitude and its benefits at any stage on our spiritual path. Gratitude makes our heart joyous. It has a calming influence as we are in contact with our deeper nature and focusing on what we *receive* rather than what we

> *Gratitude makes our heart joyous.*
> *It has a calming influence as we are in*
> *contact with our deeper nature and*
> *focusing on what we* receive *rather than*
> *what we* do *on our particular path.*
> *Gratitude soothes and evens out the*
> *choppy internal waves of anxiety and*
> *feelings of grasping or wanting.*

do on our particular path. Gratitude soothes and evens out the choppy internal waves of anxiety and feelings of grasping or wanting.

Resistances to Gratitude

There are several resistances or blocks that can limit our contact with our heart's gratitude. These are abandonment, isolation, and mistrust.

Abandonment

There will be times in nearly everyone's life when we feel abandoned by someone important. Typically, we experience our first sense of abandonment as infants. This is not to say that we had inattentive caregivers. No caregiver can be perfect. They may be struggling with satisfying their own needs and not be able to meet our infant needs. Later in life, most people experience abandonment by friends, family, or lovers. This, too, is typical. It does not mean these people had bad intentions toward us. Probably they were going through their own life changes, which resulted in a change in the relationship.

Nonetheless, these abandonment experiences can leave us with a belief that we are unlovable. In exploring this issue, we are orienting toward the truth that we have been abandoned and it has affected us in particular ways.

What is your history with abandonment?

_____

_____

_____

How do feelings of abandonment show up for you?

_____

_____

_____

Why do feelings of abandonment arise for you?

_____

_____

_____

Isolation

I am using the term "isolation" for the times in our lives when we feel aloneness without choosing to be alone. "Isolation" is a feeling of being cut off or removed from others when we very much want to be connected.

Someone who has experienced isolation frequently may believe that the isolation is justified. We can develop an internal story about how unlovable, unpleasant, or even worthless we are. When these negative internal stories are truly believed, they can become a part of our self-image we cannot see and therefore cannot question. This is where the isolation exercise can help.

What is your history with isolation?

_____

_____

_____

How do feelings of isolation show up for you?

_____

_____

_____

Why do feelings of isolation arise for you?

_____

_____

_____

Mistrust

Mistrust develops in our young lives when someone, or something, we value is taken away unexpectedly. This can be the loss of a caregiver, someone's love, or an important possession. If this happens many times, we may begin to see the world as an unstable place and mistrust whatever we identify as the source of all life. As a result, we turn away from the natural abundance life can offer because of mistrust. Fully understanding our relationship and life experience with mistrust can help us to make deeper contact with inherent trust.

What is your history with mistrust?

_____

_____

_____

How does mistrust show up for you?

_____

_____

_____

Buddha's Heart

Why does mistrust arise for you?

_____

_____

_____

Now that you have explored your relationship with the resistances to gratitude, try the gratitude practice below.

Gratitude Practice

> Sit yourself in a comfortable position in a chair or on a meditation cushion.

> Place your hands in your lap or high on your thighs.

> Close your eyes.

> Take some deep, easy belly breaths, allowing your awareness to settle within.

> Let go of thoughts, emotions, and memories.

> Direct your awareness to your heart area.

> Begin saying externally or internally one thing you are grateful for in this very moment.

Gratitude for People

Examples of what you might say include the following:

> "I am grateful for this particular person in my life since they listen to me and support my dreams."
> "I am grateful to have the home I live in to protect me and help keep me safe."
> "I am grateful for my work, which lets me share my gifts with the world."
> "I am grateful for my daily food and drink, which sustain my body."
> "I am grateful for living in a place with trees and lakes, which soothe my soul."
> "I am grateful for my health, which allows me to engage my life."
> "I am grateful for this teacher or other mentor who shares teaching with me."

Gratitude for Life's Gifts

Examples of what you may say include the following:

> "I am grateful that I have a comfortable chair or couch upon which to sit."

> "I am grateful for having a place to live."
> "I am grateful for the quiet in this room."
> "I am grateful to have good enough health to sit here now and just breathe."
> "I am grateful to have my work that helps sustain me."
> "I am grateful for the warmheartedness I feel right now."
> "I am grateful for the love and tenderness I feel in my heart."
> "I am grateful to be alive."

How was that? Was it easy or challenging for you to connect with your gratitude? Did you notice any patterns regarding the people or gifts of life that you felt gratitude for?

_____

_____

_____

These exercises can be repeated multiple times. Each time we undertake the exercises, we uncover more unconscious material from our psyche. This, in turn, helps us develop greater understanding of how our internal self-image was formed. We can also update our self-image by more thoroughly understanding what happened in our life and how we were affected. As we contact greater depths of gratitude, we open ourselves to receiving greater abundance.

Now that we are starting to understand our history with and resistances to gratitude, it is a good time to turn our practice to forgiveness. Cultivating a forgiveness practice helps us identify and release deep places of hurt and heart pain.

10

Forgiveness

PART OF WHAT OCCLUDES or masks our naturally tender heart is the memories of hurting and feeling deeply hurt by ourselves and others. When they're layered over our heart area, the guilt, remorse, anger, and judgment from suppressing hurt can lead us to feel numb. This numbness settles between our awareness and our tenderheartedness. Holding old hurts can prevent us from fully feeling the depths and capacity of our heart. One way we can begin to recognize and soften this dense layering covering our heart is through the practice of forgiveness.

Resistances to Forgiveness

Most of the resistances to forgiveness—to releasing our memories of harm, rejection, or abandonment—are intertwined with our self-identity. These resistances include believing we deserve others' harm, identifying with our anger, identifying with our hatred, and maintaining our self-definition as someone who is innocent, pure, and good.

> *Holding old hurts can prevent us from fully feeling the depths and capacity of our heart. One way we can begin to recognize and soften this dense layering covering our heart is through the practice of forgiveness.*

The Belief That We Deserve Others' Harm

Unbeknownst to us, we can create and maintain a deeply held belief that we are deserving of others' harm, rejection, or abandonment. In effect, we can have a need to only see others who harm us as being blameless. The instances and experiences of harm, rejection, and abandonment likely began in our early years. At that time, we were understandably dependent upon our caregivers for our very life. We also had a need to see them as benevolent. If instead we saw them as mean-spirited or cruel, it could cause us to become deeply ungrounded since we could not trust we would be cared for, fed, or housed. Our very lives depended upon the reliability of our caregivers. It is easier for a young child to believe they are the cause of the caregiver's harmful actions than it is to recognize the dysfunction of the caregiver.

What is your history with the belief you deserve others' harm?

_____

_____

_____

How does this belief show up for you?

_____

_____

_____

Why does this belief arise for you?

_____

_____

_____

Anger

A child can internalize their caregiver's harm by fanning the flames of anger. In a misguided way, we may feel we are punishing the caregiver by keeping the anger alive in us, as well as reclaiming our lost internal sense of lovability, competence, or personal power.

What is your history with anger?

_____

_____

_____

How does anger show up for you?

_____

_____

_____

Why does anger arise for you?

_____

_____

_____

Hatred

Hatred usually reveals itself in thoughts about seriously harming or eliminating someone from our life in response to their harming us. Hatred can feel overwhelming aggressive or as a feeling of ice-cold control.

What is your history with hatred?

_____

_____

_____

How does hatred show up for you?

_____

_____

_____

Why does hatred arise for you?

_____

_____

_____

Good, Pure, and Innocent Self-Image

We each believe that, deep down, we are really good and purely innocent. This viewpoint supports our ability to maintain a relationship with a caregiver who has harmed us. Again, we feel, at this young age, that our very survival depends upon our staying close to our life-giving caretaker.

We may attempt to maintain our internal sense of goodness and purity by replaying memories of harm, rejection, and abandonment while casting ourselves in the role of the innocent and pure one. The memories themselves become part of our internal storytelling that buttresses our sense of being good and pure.

What is your history of imagining yourself as good, pure, and innocent?

_____

_____

_____

How does this innocent self-image show up for you?

_____

_____

Why does this innocent self-image arise for you?

In my younger years, I was one of those people who, on the surface, appeared understanding and accepting. Beneath that public façade, I was holding back anger and deep shame. I had a keen memory of each instance when I had been hurt or had hurt another. I would replay those scenes regularly to my dismay. I was a captive to my painful past. It was only when I discovered and then committed to a forgiveness practice that I began to release some of these memories of hurt and felt lighter, less contracted, and more open to myself and others. I was finally starting to let go of self-judgments for the hurt I had caused, as well as anger and mistrust toward those who had hurt me, and I developed a greater understanding of why and how those hurtful interactions had happened. In an ancient Buddhist text, the *Dhammapada*, is this line:

"Hatred never ceases by hatred, but by love alone is healed. This is an ancient truth." (I recommend Gil Fronsdal's 2006 translation if you are interested in reading more.)

We will explore a series of forgiveness exercises now, loosely adapted from Jack Kornfield's forgiveness meditation. I am indebted to Jack, both for his permission to include these profound teachings and for leading the way by example for so many lay teachers in the West.

There are three parts to this practice. In the first part, we seek forgiveness for having harmed, abandoned, or rejected others. In the second, we seek forgiveness for how we have turned away from, abandoned, or harmed ourselves. In the third, we offer forgiveness to those we feel abandoned, harmed, or turned away from us.

Forgiveness Practice

For each of these exercises, do the following:

> Sit yourself in a comfortable position in a chair or on a meditation cushion.
> Place your hands in your lap or high on your thighs.
> Close your eyes.

> Take some deep, easy belly breaths, allowing your awareness to settle within.

> Let go of thoughts, emotions, and memories.

> Direct your awareness to your heart area.

Forgiveness for Having Harmed, Abandoned, or Rejected Others

Repeat out loud:

There are many ways I have harmed, abandoned, or rejected others, knowingly and unknowingly.

There have been countless times I have caused harm, abandoned others, or rejected others close to me.

I remember each of these instances now.

I have harmed, abandoned, or rejected others through my ignorance, confusion, or fear.

I humbly ask their forgiveness for my actions.

Please forgive me.

In the next part of the practice, we make contact with the harm we have caused ourselves, release our guilt or remorse, and seek forgiveness for our behavior.

Forgiveness for Having Harmed, Abandoned, or Rejected Ourselves

Repeat out loud:

There have been countless ways I have harmed, abandoned, and rejected myself, knowingly and unknowingly.
I remember these instances now.
I have harmed, rejected, or abandoned myself through my ignorance, confusion, or fear.
I humbly ask forgiveness for my actions.
I forgive myself.
May I be forgiven.

In the final step, we offer forgiveness for others who have harmed, rejected, or abandoned us.

*Forgiveness for Those Who Have Harmed,
Abandoned, or Rejected Us*

Repeat out loud:

There are many ways I have felt harmed,
rejected, or abandoned by others.

I see now this was done out of their
ignorance, confusion, or fear.

I remember these instances now.

I recall the harm, rejection, and abandonment I received.

I am ready to witness and release
these deep feelings of harm, rejection, and
abandonment.

I humbly offer forgiveness to those who I
feel have harmed, abandoned, or rejected me.

I release my deep hurt places, my memories of anger, and my memories of hatred
toward others.

I will never close my heart.

Gently breathe into your heart area.
Release everything.

Buddha's Heart

Feel your heart tenderness, feel your openness,
and embrace the joy of release, of freedom.

Breathe in your inherent purity. Feel your heart's
openness.

How was that? Was it easy or challenging for you to
connect with forgiveness for yourself or others? Did
you notice any patterns regarding the experiences or
memories of harm, rejection, or abandonment?

_____

_____

_____

11

Oneness of Reality

UNITY IS ONE POTENTIAL EXPERIENCE or realization we can have on the Buddhist path. By "Unity," I mean an undivided and merged Oneness, the origin of all form and formlessness, without a tangible form or discernable structure. From the perspective of Unity, there is a felt sense that there is an internal, authentic sameness in the essence of each of us. This does not mean each of us is the same in every way. Rather our deepest qualities are of the same source—the Absolute and the Presence of the Absolute. Yet the form qualities—the outer and inner personal qualities— are completely unique and profoundly special. In reality, there will never be a person on this planet who is exactly like you.

For twenty years, starting from my late teens, I was active in Zen Buddhist practices. I was desperate to be enlightened. I felt that if I could only locate and claim ownership of my enlightenment, all my worries, personal problems, and unskillful behavior that hurt me or others would vanish. I was myopically focused on getting my enlightenment and fantasized about dropping every aspect of my personhood and personality. This would be my salvation. At that time, I was very grounded both in my head, through intellectualism and conceptualizing, and in my belly, which solidified and grounded intuitive knowing. There was not enough heart included in my spiritual practice and life. As my spiritual understanding deepened, I witnessed myself being less run by my personality. Yet I continued to unskillfully hurt others and myself through my ignorance about my heart, the impact of my unattuned words and actions, and my unconscious self-centeredness.

Fortunately, I stumbled upon teachings pointing to a variety of useful heart practices. Once I began to specifically invite my heart area, tenderness, and inherent sweetness into my spiritual practice and life, I started to feel the inclusion of the innate wholeness of humanity, all of life itself. As I cultivated deeper heart qualities, my meditative practice expanded dramatically, leading to an awakening experience at age twenty-eight. (I do not say, "I had this experience." There is no ownership or possession of the awakening or realization experiences on the spiritual path. These experiences simply happen in the particular location of a localized consciousness.)

I had been meditating and doing my best to develop wise behavior. I had read a book called *The Sixth Patriarch's Sutra*. In the book was the line "Produce the thought that is nowhere supported." When I read this line, it was as though a foreign object had lodged in my throat. I felt that I could not swallow it or spit it out. It was wedged in tightly. I began to meditate upon this line. I sat in meditation every chance I could, day or night. The line from the book constantly ran through my mind: "Produce the thought that is nowhere supported." I repeatedly asked myself, "How could a thought be 'nowhere supported'?" I tried using logic to think myself out of this conundrum. Predictably, that did not work.

I began to trace each of the senses (sight, hearing, taste, touch, smell) back to its origin, one by one. Maybe at its source I could find how a thought can be "nowhere supported," I reasoned. I traced sight from the perception of the eye, through the ocular nerves, and into the brain. In my brain, I found I could not locate a source for sight. It felt as though there was nothing as the source of vision. I meditatively placed a kind of marker at that first source of "no source." I continued this meditative process with each sense, trying to find the answer to the riddle, the Zen *kōan*, the spiritual paradox, my conundrum.

As I traced back the last of my senses into my brain, I again found no source as a source. When I came to the source of all the no sources with the final sense, an opening occurred. The realization was that there was no source for any sense or thought! I, as a separate me, had a source of no source. The depth of my reality was: I was "no-thing." I was not my thoughts, my senses, or my brain activity. A kind of inner explosion happened. In fact, not only was I no-thing, but everyone and everything was this same no-thing, this source of no source. Rather than experience this with any kind of panic or fear, I felt relieved. I was at ease knowing this deep truth, knowing the source of no source.

This experience, this realization, of me as no-thing did not end there. Resting in no-thingness opened further. The realization next arose that the no-thingness of which each living being shared was an expression of love, of a Oneness that included absolutely everything. Nothing was excluded from the Oneness. Everything was the source of no source at its core, absent a tangible, quantifiable self, and each individual expression of this no-thingness was an undivided Oneness of love. There was only awareness of awareness, loving, unified no-thingness as the source of no source. This was an experience of the Presence of the Absolute. In effect, this was an experience of the empty spaciousness of my true nature intertwined with the juicy heartfulness of Unity, the undivided Oneness of all reality.

Typically, this knowing of Unity happens through our heart area. It is not a thought-generated head knowing but rather a deep, intuitive heart knowing, sometimes grounded in our belly area (called the *hara* in the Zen tradition). This experience of Unity, of the sameness of source or origin, happens in its own time, when our consciousness is particularly ripe and we are seated steadily within.

Nothing was excluded from the Oneness. Everything was the source of no source at its core, absent a tangible, quantifiable self, and each individual expression of this no-thingness was an undivided Oneness of love. There was only awareness of awareness, loving, unified no-thingness as the source of no source.

To more fully understand and explore our relationship to Unity, it is helpful to identify and open to the resistances that block or limit our contact with Unity.

Resistances to Unity

We can find several resistances as we begin the Unity meditation, such as a strong belief in our separateness, the feeling that maintaining no boundaries is risky (strong defenses are important), and the idea that opening ourselves to being directly in contact with Unity (a merged state) carries potential for harm.

The Belief in Our Separateness

Most aspects of our sense of self—the manner in which we internally reference and know ourselves—lead us to conclude we are a separate human being. For example, we know ourselves based upon the boundary of our body. We have learned since infancy that pain for this body does not happen outside this body. Nor are hunger, thirst, or tiredness happening anywhere else but in this body. We have our own thoughts, memories, and emotions. From these personal experiences, we conclude we are exclusively this body and it is absolutely separate from all other bodies.

Deep within our psyche is a survival instinct. The survival instinct operates to keep us safe and, most importantly, alive. Part of this survival instinct is reaffirming that our body is fine and not at risk of harm. When we cannot sense or feel part of our body or our usual array of thoughts, our survival instinct is activated. Our heart rate increases, adrenaline is activated, and breathing becomes more rapid when our survival instinct is triggered.

As we approach experiences of Unity, of merged Beingness, our body boundaries soften, our thoughts slow, our heart rate soothes, and breath quiets. This softening, soothing, and quiet typically triggers the survival instinct because our normal ways of self-referencing our body are more elusive to detect. The survival instinct treats this as an attack and activates a mental panic mode. When we are in panic mode, we are not settled, we are not open, we are not curious. We are closed in active defense.

In spiritual practice, each of us needs to experience the activation of the survival instinct repeatedly. Each time our consciousness discovers a new, deeper territory of meditative experience, our survival instinct will be activated as the new insight or realization fades. This is expected and predictable. Yet each time the survival instinct is activated following a deep meditative experience, we can see we actually were not harmed. We survived. Repeated acquaintance with deep meditative experience builds trust that we are fundamentally okay. In effect, we learn to have increased comfort moving outside our perception of ourselves.

What is your history of feeling established as a separate self?

_____

_____

_____

How do these feelings of a clearly delineated self show up for you?

_____

_____

_____

Why does this feeling of separateness arise for you?

_____

_____

_____

The Belief That Maintaining No Boundaries Is Risky

As infants and young children, we want just the right amount of connection, contact, and interaction with caregivers and family. Too much can be as problematic as too little. Most of us have had overbearing, intrusive experiences with caregivers who paid us constant attention during childhood. That type of experience translates into a feeling of invasion that sometimes leads to a sensitivity whenever we feel someone is getting too close or trying to merge with us when we are not ready. When this happens repeatedly in life, we develop a heightened defense whenever we feel we are being invaded emotionally or psychologically. We escape by beginning to shut down and collapse in on ourselves.

On the spiritual journey, there are many times when our boundaries soften, even fade temporarily, and our survival instinct is activated. Part of our journey when we feel alarmed is to test whether we really are at risk. This testing allows us to recognize that not all relaxing and merging of our boundaries is problematic or harmful.

What is your history of feeling uneasy about a threat to your personal boundaries?

_____

_____

_____

How do these feelings of threatened inner boundaries show up for you?

_____

_____

_____

Why do these feelings arise for you?

_____

_____

_____

The Belief That a Merged State Would Be Unsafe

As discussed above, in some families there was a propensity for the caregivers to regularly over merge. The caregivers were motivated by love to connect with us as children. Yet the caregivers' own neediness propelled them to constantly merge with us. These persistent caregivers wore down our boundaries and forced us to merge with them. We surrendered our boundaries and reluctantly merged with the caregiver. In the process of this merging with our caregivers, they might have lashed out or harmed us when we were in a merged, deeply connected place with them. This was likely because our caregiver felt the merged state was unsatisfying. Merging with us failed to fill the need they were feeling. This can be traumatic for a child. As a defense to this over-merging harm, the child—and later adult—can develop a belief, based on prior experience, that surrendering boundaries and merging with another is harmful and unsafe. This belief, when activated by a developing merged state, triggers our survival instinct. When the survival instinct is triggered, we shut down and try to escape mentally and/or physically.

On the spiritual journey, we will need to explore and confront our relationship with any belief that a merged state is always going to hurt. We gently challenge this belief by inviting a small merged, intimate experience. We then check to reveal whether the merging really hurt.

When our meditation deepens, offering us a new experience, it is likely our personal boundaries will be surpassed. Moving outside our normal boundaries of self can trigger our survival instinct. Our personality feels threatened by the expansiveness of our experience. We can then explore and investigate to see if it is true that we were merged within our meditative experience and check where any harm resulted. When we repeatedly confirm nothing harmful happened to us in that merged meditative experience, we gain more trust in the merged state. Gaining more trust in the merged experience recalibrates our learned beliefs about the risk of the merging.

What is your history of feeling a forced merging?

_____

_____

_____

How do these feelings of being forced to merge show up for you?

_____

_____

Why do these feelings arise for you?

_____

_____

_____

Unity Practice

> Start with the Innate Goodness Practice
> on page 58.

> Be seated in a comfortable position.

> Close your eyes.

> Place your hands comfortably on your thighs
> or in your lap.

> Allow your awareness to rest in the general
> area of your heart.

> Silently repeat, "What am I?" as you maintain
> awareness in your heart area. When responses
> arise, notice them and let them fade away.
> For example, you could hear/feel the response
> "I am my emotions." Notice and accept that

response while releasing it. As other responses arise, notice each of them and let them slip away. With sustained practice, your heart area will be openly quiet, still, and peaceful.

> Eventually it may feel more comfortable to shorten the phrase "What am I?". I do not recommend using the word "I" as a shortened expression for the entire phrase. The word "I" is convoluted, as it is infused with everything we take our "I" to be. It is advisable to use "am" for the shortened phrase. Breathe into your heart area and let the word "am" wash over you and your heart. Let yourself be deeply touched by the process.

With this sustained meditation, you may find that your sense of yourself—self-image, body boundaries—seems to soften, even fade. This is a natural by-product of this meditation. Your thoughts may become lighter, silkier, like clouds floating across the sky. Allow all of this to be present without changing or holding on to the experience.

It is a potential of this meditation to feel qualities of an undivided heart. By "undivided heart," I mean a heart that perceives itself and others as an undivided wholeness in expressing the fabric of reality. This would include witnessing trees, animals, rocks, and everything we can see as an undivided unity with what is in our heart. There is an undivided Oneness in our inner and outer perception. We can call this an experience of Unity.

This is the truth revealed in our heart's awareness. It is the complete Unity of the Presence of the Absolute. The Absolute in its sheer Presence is an undivided wholeness of merging, melting love.

How was that? Was it easy or challenging for you to connect with the merged feeling of Unity? Did you notice any patterns regarding the experiences or memories of merging or Unity?

_____

_____

_____

Culmination

IN CHAPTER 12, I provide an example of the spontaneous arising of the heart qualities of our deeper nature, so we might better understand the significance of the functioning of these heart practices in life. We experience many difficult, unexpected situations in life. We can struggle to find a response. We want to do or offer something by way of support and comfort, but we do not know the right thing to do. This is when we can tune into our heart, begin the innate goodness practice, and be open to our heart's informative wisdom.

In turning toward our innate goodness, we are choosing to orient toward the Absolute realm, the source of all creation and Beingness, which I describe more fully in Chapter 13. Our innate goodness connects us to ourselves, to others, and to the Source. This turning toward the Absolute realm relaxes our habituated movement, so we can find the right thought for a solution to the problem at hand. By turning our awareness toward the Absolute realm, we are offering ourselves. We are surrendering and conceding we do not know what to do or when to do it. Not only does this empty our mind of the need to know, we also open to the richness of not knowing. In being with not knowing, we open a territory within that contains rich possibilities. By resting in not knowing while making contact with spacious inner awareness, we can receive the wisdom of the Absolute realm, revealing what can be skillfully said or done.

12

Tenderheartedness

THROUGH THE REPEATED engagement of the practices in this book, you will more readily identify and gently relax the resistances to your true nature's heart qualities. You will become much more open to the spontaneous arising of your heart's wisdom through the practice of *upekkhā* (equanimity), *muditā* (empathetic joy), *karuṇā* (compassion), and *mettā* (loving-kindness).

One example from my life of the spontaneous arising of the *brahmavihāras* occurred when I had a dear Buddhist friend unexpectedly end up in a coma. He was suffering unending seizures. He was on very strong pain medication to minimize the brain activity causing the seizures. His family invited me to join them at the hospital. As I prepared to travel there, I turned to these heart practices.

I thought that sending my friend *mettā* would be appropriate for his circumstance. But each time I began to picture his face in my heart and develop a felt sense of his innate goodness, the practice shifted to *upekkhā*. I tried to return to *mettā* a number of times as I was fairly convinced this was the right practice for his situation.

After the fourth or fifth time the *mettā* practice shifted itself, I got the message that *upekkhā* was the right practice for my friend's dire situation. I continued the *upekkhā* practice as I travelled.

Upon arriving at the hospital, I was informed that he effectively had no functional brain activity. His body could be maintained by machines indefinitely. His family gathered in a conference room to decide the next steps. We had a frank and open discussion, with occasional tears, about keeping him on life support or removing the breathing tubes.

We each shared how we were feeling and how we felt our friend or family member would wish for us to act in these very difficult circumstances. It was unanimous that he would want all artificial life support removed.

I was one of the few people who stayed with our friend as the tubes were removed. I quietly chanted the Buddhist precepts and explained to him what was happening. Those present shared some personal feelings for him. He passed away a few minutes later.

I learned from this experience that when our heart is sufficiently tenderized and opened by these deep, transformational heart practices, our deepest true nature will inform us what is best for a particular situation.

The point of my story here is to underscore that all the meditative practices and exercises in this book are intended to orient and activate your contact with your heart's true nature. Because we are complex beings with involved psychologies and life experiences, we need a variety of spiritual practices to help us see through our conventional ideas about ourselves and to release our hurt places and painful memories. As we engage with and deepen the practices in this book, we increasingly open our inner heart, the universal heart of deep inclusive love, with its quality of sweetness and complete acceptance. Our deepening contact with the unconditioned love in our heart opens our ripening

> *Our deepening contact with the unconditioned love in our heart opens our ripening consciousness to the heart of the Universe, the heart of Presence. This is a heart that provides us with our life force energy, our creative spirit, our deepest dreams, our greatest capacity to receive love.*

consciousness to the heart of the Universe, the heart of Presence. This is a heart that provides us with our life force energy, our creative spirit, our deepest dreams, our greatest capacity to receive love.

This is the awakening of the heart, the grounding in the Buddha's Heart.

13

Absolute View

TO MORE FULLY UNDERSTAND the Buddha's heart, it is useful to include, and explore, the source of this heart. This source encompasses all the meditations, practices, and exercises we have explored. It is the source for all religions and spiritual practices.

What I am presenting here is ultimate reality. A reality anchored in the Source of all reality—the Absolute. I am presenting not only some of what I see in each realm but also the experiential felt sense of the Absolute to afford the reader potential contact with this reality.

For the novice practitioner, many of these ideas and concepts will be foreign. To the new reader, this may seem akin to science fiction. Yet I encourage all to read this chapter. One of my early Zen teachers told me, when I received teaching that sounded more imaginative to me at that time, to "put it on the back burner." She encouraged me not to throw out what I did not yet understand but instead to hold it as a maybe and let my developing meditation experiences inform my understanding. This advice was more profound and life altering than I then knew.

For the established Buddhist practitioner, it is important to fully understand the source, the inspiration, of all the meditations in this book. Being clear about the source— Absolute reality—affords the reader greater access to the grounding and brilliant wisdom embedded and expressed in these timeless yet ancient Buddhist meditations.

> *Being clear about the source— Absolute reality—affords the reader greater access to the grounding and brilliant wisdom embedded and expressed in these timeless yet ancient Buddhist meditations.*

Each step or stage of this progression and practice from the Absolute realm through our everyday personality is presented, as much as is possible here, from my experiential realizations, my work with my teachers, and my direct interactions with my students.

We will start from the territory of the Absolute realm, also called "the Absolute." The Absolute functions far beyond the reaches of any conceptual understanding. It is infinite without particularity as to space, time, or hierarchical development. That means that no experience or realization is truly superior or progressively better than any other insight, understanding, or realization. Our awareness enters the Absolute by being completely merged with the Absolute. In this merging, the Absolute recognizes itself in our awareness. The Absolute is always beyond conventional thought and conceptual understanding. This Absolute reality is infused with and in consensual, normal, everyday reality.

The Absolute realm is the source of all creation. In the Absolute realm, there are no conditions, no polarities of opinion, no preferences, no language, no thoughts, and no concepts, as everything is lovingly included. It is a unified, infinite Oneness of reality. Dual concepts such as right and wrong, me and you, subject and object do not exist separately from the Absolute. This is a unified Oneness that lovingly contains and initiates everything, while excluding nothing. Paradoxically, it contains nothing in addition to containing everything. It is a dark, vast, infinite, mysterious Presence. We will never know every mystery enfolded in the Absolute realm. It is profound peace spread over a vast spaciousness. This peacefulness has a resonating quality of powerful, reverberating silence. Its peacefulness, its profound silent power, is all love. It is an encompassing, welcoming, non-judgmental love. Love is the medium of the Absolute realm and all of reality. The love here is profoundly striking in its quality of multilayered depths. It is intensely impactful to experience the subtle nuance of the profound resonance here. It is nearly overwhelming to touch into the multilayered knowing enfolded in this realm. Yet it also feels simple and soothing to abide here, resting as the Absolute.

Imagine yourself deeply inside a dark, vast, infinite space. It is so vast that awareness cannot feel or sense any edge or end point in this boundless space. Awareness is floating in deep, still outer space. There is no sound. Every thought, emotion, or memory of you and your life has been thoroughly absorbed by this profound, loving stillness. You feel no body perceptions, body boundaries, or any mode of identity. Awareness here has no location. The spacious, still Presence is everything you are. There is no discomfort, suffering, or emotional pain. Breathing in and out, without awareness of a body, expresses enveloping, engulfing peace. Awareness is interconnected with the Presence here. There is no need to alter anything or to get anywhere. Nothing is needed. There is complete, thorough contentment. The penetrating contentment abides here with its deeply felt sense of undivided connection with welcome, loving

Beingness. Everything is content as it is all the same source, an identical Oneness. When our individual consciousness meets this profound infinite peace, consciousness slowly quiets and stills. Thought ceases. Concepts fall away without the repetition of thoughts. Consciousness itself, functioning as awake awareness, stops. It utterly ceases. The ceasing of consciousness in this profound, still, loving peace is called "Cessation." It is the cessation of *all* consciousness.

Cessation of consciousness is not an experience of absence or loss but of an open, still fullness. It is an experience of directly knowing the profound and richly layered mystery. Cessation is only known after the awareness of consciousness has moved out of Cessation and back into the fullness of the Absolute realm. There is a particular quality of nonconceptual, intuitive knowing that deeply understands Cessation as the source of all creation, all awareness, all consciousness. There is a profound impact through merging with the deep territory of the Absolute realm. Cessation is nirvana/*nibbāna*, the alpha and omega of every form of reality.

The Absolute contains all levels and depths of awakening as well as all types of realization without preferencing any particular spiritual practice, tradition, or religion. The Absolute is the undifferentiated, sole source of all religions, spiritual schools, and associated practices. The Absolute has no preferences or favorites. It is the source of all reality. This is a realm that is before any form appears out of the vastness. It is without self-images, concepts, or mental structures. It contains, and is, the unified whole. This is a realm of Being, of the Beingness of the Absolute. The felt sense is of deep contentment without discernment as to preference or effort to establish any type of priority or hierarchy of experience. Yet this unimaginable formless source can only express itself in form, in manifestation. It is through manifestation that awareness can return to the Absolute realm and to its unmanifest source—Cessation. This realm contains a quality of objective identity. There is no particular subject or object. There is no vantage point of a me perceiving or observing in the Absolute realm. There is a knowing of perception in these realms without thought or any mental activity. Because there is no perception of anything resembling a self or anything separate to perceive, we call this a "nondual" state. The Formless Realms, including the Absolute realm, afford our consciousness/soul the opportunity to realize limitless, unbounded reality without a particular felt sense of self or even a perspective of a self. There is a benefit of soothing relaxation in our soul when we do not need to maintain and animate a separate sense of self or a perception of this self. We are deeply relaxed when resting in the natural union with, and as, the Absolute realm.

Base of Neither Perception Nor Non-Perception

The Absolute begins its move toward worldly form in gradations, steps emanating from a still source first to the nonconceptual realm. This realm is referred to in Buddhism as the Base of Neither Perception Nor Non-Perception. This is a clear paradox. There is no perception we can identify with, or as, yet there is some wisp of perception/awareness. There is truly no perception and no non-perception here. This is the first realm of reality where the Absolute will present itself in its journey toward everyday form. These first four realms are called the "Formless Realms." I use the term "realm" specifically because the felt sense is one of a specific territory, a functioning and wholesome reality, that is complete and separate from other realms of reality. The Base of Neither Perception Nor Non-Perception is a realm in which there is no typical manner of perception and also no non-perception or lack of perception. We will have a nonlocalized awareness here. A "nonlocalized awareness" means there is an expansive awareness that does not have a particular location from which it is oriented or rooted. Yet there is an awareness within the realm itself. Having non-ordinary perception without our usual ability or habit of perception is intellectually confounding. This is an unresolvable paradox that simply must be accepted through direct experience. It is only through experiential contact, temporarily abiding and being merged in this rich, remarkable, unparalleled realm, that its reality can be experienced. Awareness is completely merged in this perception of non-perception. Each of these Formless Realms has the potential to be an ongoing teaching, an open conduit of learning and of direct knowing, that can continue well after the meditative participation in the particular realm has concluded. If there is sufficient sustained immersion in the particular Formless Realm, a portal remains open—informing and teaching.

Base of No-Thing-Ness

From the Base of Neither Perception Nor Non-Perception, the Absolute, in its journey toward everyday reality, or consensual reality, manifests as the Base of Nothingness. It might be better understood as being experienced as No-Thing-Ness, rather than Nothing or Nothingness. Nothingness suggests an absence, a lack, a vacuum that is yet to be filled. This concept of "yet to be filled" is not experientially accurate in this realm. This is a realm where there is a full, expansive No-Thing-Ness profoundly manifesting. It is not an absence of any kind. It is a complete realm containing the infinite space of No-Thing-Ness that will ultimately hold and contain the realm of all of consciousness, every manifestation, all forms of reality. This is a realm where we can abide in, and as, an absence that is full—pregnant with potentiality, with no signs, mental markers, or qualities of self-identity. The felt sense here is of a vast Openness similar to the potency of a blank canvas about to be overlaid with vibrant representations of the abundant colors of life. It is profoundly quiet. Still peacefulness soothes our awareness while refreshingly cleansing our preference for life's movement of activity.

The Base of No-Thing-Ness does not contain the magnificent potential of the Absolute realm, where anything and everything can arise at any time. In the Base of No-Thing-Ness, there is already a movement toward consciousness, toward everyday life. This movement toward everyday life conditions this realm with subtle purpose—to hold what will manifest or come into creation. In contrast, the Absolute realm has no conditions and contains both the potential of what will manifest and what will never manifest.

Base of Boundless Consciousness

From the Base of No-Thing-Ness, the Absolute next appears, in its journey toward the world of form and manifestation, as the Base of Boundless Consciousness.

The Base of Boundless Consciousness is a realm that, while still objectively pristine in itself, can be known to be held by the Base of No-Thing-Ness, which can be known to be held by the Base of Neither Perception Nor Non-Perception, which are all held by the Absolute realm. All are different yet related expressions of the Absolute, the source of all.

The Base of Boundless Consciousness holds and expresses everything in the world of form, manifestation, structure, idea, thought, concept, even belief and opinion. Yet it holds these in a profoundly still, powerful silence. The Base of Boundless Consciousness is a rich, alive fullness. It is the deep silence and pristine stillness of the Base of No-Thing-Ness opening, flowering, moving toward and into manifestation, in its resplendent form.

The felt sense here is one of life energy poised to open into everyday reality. It feels like a seed that has been germinating in rich soil and is just about to reach out of the earth toward the sun and sky with the first stretch of its leaves.

The experiential sense is of the potentiality of pure aliveness preparing to bud and flower.

Base of Boundless Space

From the Base of Boundless Consciousness, the Absolute, moving toward everyday reality, manifests as the Base of Boundless Space. This realm is space without boundary, limitation, form, or restriction. It is simply silent vastness stretching to infinity yet contained wholly in the smallest subatomic particle. This realm of Boundless Space is needed if the world of form is to exist. All form is held in, and by, the boundless quality of this space and by the Absolute functioning, brilliantly manifesting, as the Base of Boundless Space.

Resting in this infinite, formless space is soothing and rejuvenating. There is no form yet. It is free of constriction or definition here. Our awareness is merged with this vast, formless, pristine space expanding in every direction without any potential for limitation. We are free here from allegiance to any form, any label, any concept or idea. That freedom is nourishing to our consciousness and awareness. We can put everything down as we release into, and abide as, this infinite space.

Form World

From the Base of Boundless Space, the Absolute begins to manifest in the form world richly as colors and tangibly as earthly elements (earth, water, fire, and wind). These earthly elements and rich, complex colors transform the luminous blackness of the Absolute into the forms and structures we know in our ordinary, everyday perception and awareness. From the Formless Realms, moving toward the form world, the Absolute appears as what we can call our "true nature."

True Nature

Our true nature is our deepest, most subtle, essential self. This is not a self of personality but rather an awareness that is not born and does not die. Our true nature contains a variety of qualities, such as compassion, love, peace, joy, stillness, strength, power, etc., that are without condition— universally available to all. This means you do not need to *do* anything for these qualities to appear. You do not need to behave a certain way or hold a certain viewpoint for these qualities to naturally, spontaneously arise in your awareness as your deepest nature. These qualities are already embedded in our consciousness, a kind of spiritual, holographic

DNA with us from birth. These are not emotional or mental structures or states, nor do they arise as a result of any kind or type of doing. Qualities of our true nature are manifested by, and through, our Beingness, our ability to simply be who we are before we solidify, or structure, into believing we are exclusively a particular mentalized personality.

When we are intimate with our present-moment experience, without reactivity or a personality "doing," these qualities of true nature can, and will, spontaneously arise. The qualities of true nature will be spontaneous and freely attuned to meet our needs, known and unknown. We can have experiences and contact with our true nature throughout our spiritual/meditative/contemplative life. Contact with qualities of our true nature collect—even compound—in our consciousness, which supports a developing inner knowing, spiritual awakenings, and later sustained functioning realizations. There are unlimited realizations that are within the potentiality of the Absolute. All realizations awaken in our aware consciousness, never in our personality. We can never retain or possess experiences of realization. What allows the realization to be experienced in our consciousness is the absence, the transparency, of our normal personality self. This transparency of self allows our awareness to be without limits, unrestricted in its connection with the mysterious qualities and in all manifestations of the Absolute.

No-Self and Absence of Self

There is a range of awakening experience between our usual self, the absence of self, and the profound, empty fullness of no-self. "Absence of self" is when our normal sense of self is temporarily suspended through its transparency. The ways in which we self-reference—from our belief in the permanence of our body boundaries to the conviction in our abiding emotions, memories, thoughts, and mental structures—are suspended when ego transparency is present. When these become temporarily transparent, the result is that we typically have no idea who we are. There is nothing within us that is an identifier. We may perceive an inner spaciousness in place of our personality. This inner spaciousness potentially may have spontaneously arising qualities such as peace, love, compassion, clarity, or other qualities of true nature. Should the experiences of absence of self persist without a move to change or avoid it, we can experience the ripe fullness of no-self.

No-self can arise when we have a more sustained knowing that our normal self is not ultimately true. That our self is not ultimately a final truth becomes a foundational truth in itself. Our usual self is a relative truth. It is conditioned by our body boundaries, our traumas, our memories, our emotional history, our thoughts, our repetitive patterns of behavior, and our mental structures. Should there be a deep enough sustained immersion in absence of self, we can perceive the hollowness of our belief in being exclusively a self, separate from all other forms of reality, while opening to the realization that our aware, awake consciousness is in reality a no-self. This is a functioning awake awareness that does not need our history, our body, or our mental structures of identity to know who we are.

To begin opening to contact with absence of self, we start with sustained, active observing of the typical, familiar patterns of form in our body as well as the mental structures in our mind. It is important to slow down, to cultivate inner silence, to turn our awareness toward our interiority, and to not place so much awareness outside of our body. Typically, we maintain an inner and outer perception of our body. This perception is solid due in part to our firm belief that our body boundaries are an unchanging reality. In the experience of absence of self, in spiritual practice, we are questioning the reality of who we are, who we believe ourselves to be. Early in our lives, we feel need (hunger for food, attention, or love) and believe satisfaction only comes from another person outside of us when we feel pain or discomfort. This developing belief that all pleasure is generated solely by another leads us to be firmly convinced we are unable to satisfy ourselves. We believe we lack the inherent capacity to be self-satisfied in our life.

To begin to question this core belief that we are only a separate self, we use meditation as the most direct path of questioning, cutting allegiance to our conviction in an identity as an abiding separate self. The Buddha not only taught but also practiced *samatha* (concentration/tranquility meditation) as the most direct method for questioning our firm belief that we are an entity separate from all other life-forms. Throughout this book, we have questioned the conviction of a consensual reality as ultimate reality. We have applied the heart practices of concentration meditation to meet and tenderize our heart. We have undertaken these exercises, meditations, and practices while cultivating a developing orientation toward our interiority. Through an inner spaciousness, we can make contact with the vast Formless Realms of experience. This journey can open into the source of reality, the Absolute realm, containing the touchstone of all creation, Cessation. Cessation is the deepest, most mysterious heart of the unending mystery that is us and simultaneously the entirety of all universes.

Conclusion

IN THIS BOOK, you have learned and hopefully participated in a variety of meditations, exercises, and spiritual practices. We have journeyed together into the heart qualities of our deeper nature. We have naturally met and explored your particular resistances to these heart qualities. You may be wondering now: What's next?

I suggest maintaining these heart meditations and practices in your home practice. You might wish to select a particular heart practice and work with it over the course of a number of weeks or a month. By selecting just one heart meditation or practice at a time, you will penetrate more deeply into accessing that particular heart quality. I advise keeping a journal during this time. You can record both your responses to the ongoing resistance exercises, as you deepen your understanding of these resistances, and record your on-the-cushion and off-the-cushion experiences, insights, and learnings. Record how you are being affected.

Each of these meditations, practices, and exercises can be repeated regularly. There is a permeating quality to the effects of these practices. In other words, your heart will continue to open, your unskillful behavior will minimize, and you will be happier and more content overall.

Continuing this journey is assisted by two things. First, going on a retreat to spend days steeping in these heart qualities, with a supportive group and a skilled teacher, will draw you deeper into your heart while helping you understand your personality patterns and workings. I offer online retreats. These consist of prearranged meeting times for dharma talks, questions, practical exercises, periods of meditation together, and one-on-one meetings with me.

Second, working with a skilled teacher on a monthly or biweekly basis will help you illuminate the heart qualities being activated and process the learned patterns of behavior that reject our deepest heart qualities, keeping us struggling on the surface, just out of reach of contentment. For students, it is useful to experience the heart and soul resonance with a teacher who is a living expression of the Presence of the Absolute. Being in regular contact with the clarity and deep peace of this Presence encourages the student to recognize the music and flow of the universe when it is here.

I would love to work directly with you to support your deepening understanding of the heart practices and

tctntactntact me contact me through

entential.

Acknowledgments

I WOULD LIKE TO EXPRESS my profound thanks to all my teachers—past, present, and future—for their guidance and for walking their talk.

Thank you to my great team, without whom this book would not have been as polished and presentable—Carra Simpson, Erin Parker, Jazmin Welsh, and Lynn Slobogian.

Thank you to my wife, Julie; our shared children, Rachel, Ben, Ryan, Jason, and Emily; and our grandchildren, Audri, Aleah, Jade, Sienna, Sam, Collin, and Grahm, for being in my life.

About the Author

STEPHEN SNYDER began practicing daily meditation in 1976. Since then, he has studied Buddhism extensively— investigating and engaging in Theravada, Zen, and Tibetan Buddhism, as well as the Diamond Approach. Stephen was authorized to teach in 2007 by the Venerable Pa Auk Sayadaw,  a Burmese meditation master and renowned scholar. In 2009, he coauthored *Practicing the Jhānas*, exploring deep concentration meditation as presented by Pa Auk Sayadaw. In 2020, Stephen authored *Stress Reduction for Lawyers*, which supports improved relaxation, communication, and happiness by integrating simple meditation techniques into demanding careers.

Stephen's resonant and warmhearted teaching style engages students around the globe through in-person and online retreats, as well as one-on-one online coaching. He encourages students to turn toward their inherent awakened awareness and, through this realization, embody and live from their true identity. For more information, please visit www.awakeningdharma.org.

Did you benefit from Buddha's Heart?

SHARE YOUR PRAISE

Did this book help you to establish or to develop a personal meditation practice? Did it offer new insights into Buddhist teachings that are benefiting your daily life or interactions? If so, a review, shared through your favorite online retailer, would be warmly welcomed. A few minutes of your time could help others find this book and benefit as you have.

PLACE A BULK ORDER

Would you like to share this book with a group or a class? Please be in touch! We can offer bulk discounts for orders of ten or more copies to most locations. Please write to buddhasheartpress@gmail.com.

KEEP IN TOUCH

For more about Stephen's books, workshops, and other offerings, please visit www.awakeningdharma.org.

Also by Stephen Snyder

Stress Reduction for Lawyers, Law
Students, and Legal Professionals:
Learning to Relax

PAPERBACK • 978-1-7347810-0-7 • $14.95

E-BOOK • 978-1-7347810-1-4 • $9.95

PUBLISHED SEPTEMBER 2020

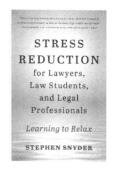

A practical guide for a more relaxed and enjoyable legal career—authored by a retired lawyer and senior meditation teacher. This book offers straightforward techniques to identify the events that cause stress in your work, apply practices that support deep relaxation, and develop greater satisfaction in your work and personal life.

Practicing the Jhānas: Traditional
Concentration Meditation as Presented
by the Venerable Pa Auk Sayadaw

PAPERBACK • 978-1-59030-733-5 • $22.95

E-BOOK • 978-0-8348-2282-5 • $17.99

PUBLISHED DECEMBER 2009

COAUTHORED WITH TINA RASMUSSEN

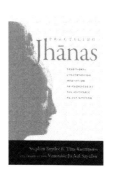

A clear and in-depth presentation of the traditional Theravada concentration meditation known as *jhāna* practice, developed from practicing *jhāna* meditation in retreat under the guidance of one of the great living meditation masters, the Venerable Pa Auk Sayadaw.

Printed in Great Britain
by Amazon

78454413R00125